ETH

Sarah

with responses from Frederic
Vivienne Bozalek, Chris Becket
Merlinda Weinberg and Paul Blackledge

SERIES EDITORS:
Iain Ferguson and Michael Lavalette

This print edition first published in Great Britain in 2014 by

Policy Press
University of Bristol
1-9 Old Park Hill
Bristol BS2 8BB
UK
t: +44 (0)117 954 5940
pp-info@bristol.ac.uk
www.policypress.co.uk

North American office:
Policy Press
c/o The University of Chicago Press
1427 East 60th Street
Chicago, IL 60637, USA
t: +1 773 702 7700
f: +1 773-702-9756
e:sales@press.uchicago.edu
www.press.uchicago.edu

ISBN 978 1 44731 618 3 Paperback

British Library Cataloguing in Publication Data
A catalogue record for this book is available from the British Library.

Library of Congress Cataloging-in-Publication Data
A catalog record for this book has been requested.

OTHER TITLES AVAILABLE IN THIS SERIES

POVERTY AND INEQUALITY by Chris Jones and Tony Novak

PERSONALISATION by Peter Beresford

ADULT SOCIAL CARE by Iain Ferguson and Michael Lavalette

MENTAL HEALTH by Jeremy Weinstein

CHILDREN AND FAMILIES by Paul Michael Garrett

For more information about this series visit: www.policypress.co.uk/
crdsw.asp

Policy Press also publishes the journal *Critical and Radical Social Work*; for
more information visit: http://www.policypress.co.uk/journals_crsw.asp

Contents

Part Three: Concluding remarks

Notes on contributors

Lead author

Professor Sarah Banks is Co-director of the Centre for Social Justice and Community Action at Durham University. She has a background in community development and previously worked in the voluntary sector and local authority social services. Her research interests include professional ethics, community development, community-based participatory research and work with young people.

Respondents

Frederic G. Reamer is Professor in the graduate program of the School of Social Work, Rhode Island College, US. His research and teaching have focused primarily on public policy, crime and criminal justice, professional ethics and social work ethics, and he has many publications in these areas. He chaired the national task force that wrote the current National Association of Social Workers Code of Ethics.

Stephen Cowden is Senior Lecturer in Social Work at the University of Coventry. His main research interests are in the areas of social work theory and practice, 'race', religion and fundamentalism and critical pedagogy. He is the author (with Annie Pullen-Sansfaçon) of *The moral and ethical foundations of social work* (Pearson-Longman, 2012).

Vivienne Bozalek is Professor of Social Work and also Director of Teaching and Learning at the University of the Western Cape (UWC), South Africa. Her areas of research, publications and expertise include the use of post-structural social justice and the political ethics of care perspectives. In 2010 she received the Association of Southern African Social Work Education Institutions (ASASWEI) Distinguished Educator of the Year Award.

Chris Beckett is a Senior Lecturer in Social Work at the University of East Anglia. He is the author of several textbooks, including *Assessment and intervention in social work* (Sage, 2010), and is a member of the editorial board of the journal *Ethics and Social Welfare*. He also has a parallel career as a writer of fiction.

Michael Reisch is the Daniel Thursz Distinguished Professor of Social Justice at the University of Maryland and one of the leading and most respected social work scholars and educators in the US. He is the author of many articles and books including *The road not taken: a history of radical social work in the United States* (with Janice Andrews) (Brunner-Routledge, 2002) and has recently edited a major collection of writings entitled *Social policy and social justice* (Sage, 2013).

Fumihito Ito is Associate Professor of Social Work at Nihon Fukushi University, Japan. He is a member of the editorial board of the journal *Critical and Radical Social Work* and was a lead contributor to the ESRC seminar series *The impact of new public management policies and perspectives on professional social work: a comparison of British and Japanese experiences* (ESRC, 2010).

Merlinda Weinberg is an assistant professor in the School of Social Work at Dalhousie University, Canada. Dr Weinberg received her MSW from Smith College in the US. Prior to becoming a social work educator, she practised social work in Canada and the US as a front-line worker, manager and consultant for over 25 years. She has written many articles and journal papers on social work ethics and around the theme of moral distress.

Paul Blackledge is Professor of Politics at Leeds Metropolitan University. He is on the editorial board of several journals, including *Historical Materialism* and *International Socialism*. His most recent research has focused on the intersection between Marxism and ethical theory. Among many other publications, he is the author of *Marxism and ethics: freedom, desire, and revolution* (SUNY Press, 2012).

Series editors

Iain Ferguson is Professor of Social Work and Social Policy at the University of the West of Scotland and a member of the Steering Committee of the Social Work Action Network.

Michael Lavalette is Professor of Social Work and Social Policy at Liverpool Hope University and National Co-ordinator of the Social Work Action Network.

Series editors' introduction

For much of its history, mainstream social work in Britain has been a fairly conservative profession. It has often reflected the dominant political ideologies of the day, while presenting itself as resolutely 'non-political'. Thus, the first social work organisation, the Charity Organisation Society (COS) (1869), rigorously adhered to the Poor Law notion that the poor could be divided into 'deserving' and 'undeserving', rejected any form of state intervention aimed at improving people's lives (including free school meals and old-age pensions) and saw the practice of individual casework as the best antidote to the spread of socialist ideas.

By contrast, social work in the 1960s reflected a broad social democratic consensus, evident in the recommendations of the Seebohm Report in England and Wales and the Kilbrandon Report in Scotland on the basis of which the new generic social work departments were established. In most respects, the social work of this period reflected a huge advance on the punitive individualism of the COS (and, it should be said, the punitive individualism of our own time). Even then, however, there was still a tendency to pathologise (albeit it was communities rather than individuals that were seen as failing) and to ignore the extent to which statutory social work intervention continued to be experienced by service users as oppressive and paternalistic. Be that as it may, the progressive possibilities of the new departments were soon cut short by the onset of a global economic crisis in 1973 to which the Labour governments of the time could offer no answer, except cuts and belt-tightening.

What is also true, however, as we have argued elsewhere (Lavalette and Ferguson, 2007), is that there has always been another tradition in social work, an activist/radical approach which has sought to present an alternative vision both to individualism and also to paternalist, top-down collectivism. This approach, which flourished in the UK in the 1970s, located the problems experienced by those who sought social work support in the material conditions of their lives and attempted to develop practice responses which challenged these conditions and their effects.

One source of theory underpinning that approach was the excellent series Critical Texts in Social Work and the Welfare State, edited by Peter Leonard and published by Macmillan.

Three decades on, this current series aims to similarly deepen and refresh the critical and radical social work tradition by providing a range of critical perspectives on key issues in contemporary social work. Social work has always been a contested profession but the need for a space for debate and discussion around ways forward for those committed to a social work practice informed by notions of social justice has never been greater. The issues are complex. How should social workers view personalisation, for example? In an era of austerity, can social work be about more than simply safeguarding and rationing scarce services? Will the integration of services in areas such as mental health lead to improved services or simply greater domination of medical models? Do social work practices offer an escape from managerialism and bureaucracy or are they simply a Trojan horse for privatisation?

These are some of the questions which contributors to this series – academics, practitioners, service users and movement activists - will address. Not all of those contributing to these texts would align themselves with the critical or radical tradition. What they have in common, however, is a commitment to a view of social work which is much wider than the currently dominant neoliberal models and a belief that notions of human rights and social justice should be at the heart of the social work project.

Ethics: Sarah Banks

Recent years have seen renewed interest in the subject of social work ethics. In the lead article in this collection, Sarah Banks argues that this can be seen as reflecting two very different agendas. On the one hand, it is part of a progressive movement which offers a critique of New Public Management (NPM) approaches through emphasising the role of social workers as active moral agents working for social justice. On

—

the other hand, the growth of interest in ethics can be viewed as part of NPM, with codes of ethics a means of regulating and controlling the conduct of professionals and service users. She emphasises the importance of reclaiming professional ethics for social work, and outlines a preliminary framework for a situated ethics of social justice.

In the Responses section, academics from a wide range of theoretical traditions and geographical locations, including the US, South Africa and Japan, discuss and debate Sarah's arguments, and the book concludes with her reply to her respondents.

Reclaiming social work ethics: challenging the new public management[1]

Sarah Banks

Introduction

In his book *Reclaiming social work*, Ferguson (2008, p 132) includes a short section entitled 'Reclaiming the ethical'. He writes in the context of increasing managerialism and marketisation in the field of social work in the late 20th and early 21st century – a period that has witnessed an erosion of practice premised on values of social justice and human dignity. This chapter is a response to Ferguson's call – made all the more urgent with the new public austerity that prevails in many countries following the financial crisis of 2008. In this climate of welfare reform and public sector restructuring, social workers are increasingly finding themselves expected to monitor and control the behaviour of the growing numbers of people who are poor, sick, disabled and stigmatised.

This article examines the growth of interest in social work ethics in the context of neoliberal policies and, in particular, the growth of managerialism in public service professions. The main characteristics of neoliberal policies are the promotion of free markets and the privatisation of public goods, along with a strengthening of private property rights and weakening of labour rights – resulting in a growing centralisation of wealth and power (Harvey, 2005). Taking the UK as an example, while drawing links with trends across Europe and other countries in the global North, the article traces the development of the 'new public management' (NPM) since the 1990s. NPM is characterised as stressing the importance of measurable outputs, targets, competition and cost-effectiveness in the provision of public services. The article considers the extent to which the growth of interest in ethics in social work is part of a progressive movement to offer a critique of NPM through emphasising the role of social workers as active moral agents working for social justice. Alternatively, the growth of interest in ethics can be viewed as part of NPM, with a focus on ethics as being about the regulation of the conduct of professionals and service users. The article concludes by emphasising the importance of reclaiming professional ethics for social work, outlining a preliminary framework for a situated ethics of social justice.

Ethics and radical social work

Ferguson's (2008) brief section on 'reclaiming the ethical' amounts to a call for social workers to resist attacks on the core values of social work. It is, in effect, a call to reassert a value base that has at its heart a profound solidarity with people who are experiencing poverty, indignity, suffering and all forms of oppression. This is one part of what 'reclaiming the ethical' means for social work – namely reasserting and arguing for a radical definition of the ethical values of social justice and empathic solidarity with the poor. These are values that have got lost in an everyday social work practice driven by market values of economy, efficiency and a concern with maintaining social order in a period of severe crisis of capitalism. The statement on ethics for direct social work developed by Slovenian social workers and academics involved in the Occupy Ljubljana movement (Flaker, 2012) is a good example of this process of reclaiming social work values (the list includes promoting advocacy for the powerless, active resistance against injustice and refusing to treat people as objects). In this sense, 'reclaiming the ethical' is a project concerned with rearticulating a set of progressive values for social work (see also Progressive Social Work Network (Hong Kong), 2011).

There is, however, another very important sense of 'reclaiming the ethical' that I also wish to consider in this article. It is about reclaiming the topic of 'ethics': reclaiming what we mean by 'the ethical'. For alongside the growth of managerialism and market-driven social welfare programmes, there has also been a growth of interest in the topic of ethics. Some of the growing concern with ethics has been in response to the erosion of the social work value base and can be seen as part of the resistance described above. However, an equally significant feature of the 'ethics boom' has been the development of ethical standards, codes and regulatory systems for controlling and disciplining professionals and the people with whom they work. Here 'the ethical' is not about resistance and radical action, but rather about conformity to prevailing social norms and regulations. So what does 'reclaiming the ethical' mean in this context? For those theorists and practitioners who identify themselves as radical (in the sense of socialist, feminist, critical or anti-oppressive, for example), it may be more about claiming ethics as part of the radical project, as much as it is about reclaiming the ethical. For ethics as a topic in its own right has tended not to feature strongly in texts on radical social work.

The literature on radical social work of the 1970s and 1980s (for example, Bailey and Brake, 1975; Corrigan and Leonard, 1978; Brake and Bailey, 1980; Galper, 1980; Langen and Lee, 1989) said very little about ethics as a topic. There may be a number of reasons for this, including the fact that interest in professional ethics as an identifiable subject area in social work was only just emerging in the 1970s (Reamer, 1999, p 7). In addition, ethics was not a topic covered explicitly by Marx, or many of the other Marxist theorists upon which the radical social work literature drew. This does not mean that in the writings of Marx himself and in the radical social work literature there is no reference to themes that we might regard as the subject matter of ethics (human needs, relationships, equality, justice), just that these are not labelled as 'ethical' themes. These themes arise as part of a political analysis of the nature of society and a political commitment

3

to striving for a better world. They arise in the context of clear value judgements about what is wrong with our current society, what counts as a good society and what people (including social workers) should do to make this better world possible. This kind of radical politics is inclusive of ethics (if we regard ethics as being about people's conduct and character relating to what is right/wrong, good/bad) but does not separate it out as an identifiable topic in its own right. This does not mean that an ethical perspective is rejected or absent, but rather that the ethics within radical politics is deeply embedded in the political analysis. As Critchley (2007, p 132) comments: 'Politics is an ethical practice that is driven by a response to situated injustices and wrongs'.

While some theorists have argued that several different and contradictory ethical positions can be found in the writings of Marx and Marxism (Kamenka, 1969; Lukes, 1985), others have argued that it is possible to identify and develop a Marxist ethics from Marx's writings (Truitt, 2005; Blackledge, 2008). But it is not in the form of a traditional Western ethical theory based on the idea of ethics as pertaining to universal (for all time and places) principles of right and wrong, enacted by abstract individual moral agents making impartial judgements. Indeed, Marx characterised this kind of rationalist, universal ethics as a bourgeois illusion (Marx and Engels, 1848/1969, pp 60, 68) – a morality (or system of ethics) which presents prevailing liberal social norms as universal and impartial (such as rights to private property and privacy), whilst in fact they serve the interests of the ruling class. As Eagleton (2011, pp 158–9) points out, when Marx denounced 'morality' this does not mean he did not have a moral (or ethical)[2] stance himself. What he was, in fact, denouncing, was 'moralism' – which abstracts moral values from their historical contexts and makes moral judgements as if based on universal standards. Underpinning Marx's writings is an ethical perspective that is situated in a specific time and economic system and takes sides with those who are oppressed and exploited (Truitt, 2005, p 13). According to Blackledge (2008, p 1), Marx offers an alternative ethics that takes as its starting point 'the collective struggles of workers against their exploitation'. It is this kind of ethical position

4

that is present in the literature on radical social work, even though it is not explicitly labelled as 'ethics'.

At a time when the ethical is increasingly associated with devising and following codified rules, with conformity to standards and with the individual making ethical judgements based on rational deduction from abstract universal principles, it is particularly important to reclaim a situated ethics, that is about values and commitments of people as social beings engaged in collective struggles for a better world.

What is ethics?

Before proceeding to document the 'ethics boom' and the rise of NPM, I will first outline how I understand the term 'ethics'. In this article I am using 'ethics' in a broad sense to refer to a subject area that covers all or some of the following themes:

- *Conduct* – what actions are regarded as right and wrong (eg promise-keeping and lying)?
- *Character* – what moral qualities are regarded as good and bad (eg. trustworthiness and deceitfulness; altruism and selfishness)?
- *Relationships* – what responsibilities attach to people's relationships with each other, individually and in groups (eg the responsibility of a parent towards a child; the responsibility of a community towards its vulnerable members)?
- *The good society* – in what kind of society do we want to live (eg a society in which all living beings flourish in harmony with the natural environment; a society in which all human beings are free to enjoy the fruits of their labour)?

This is a deliberately broad description of the subject matter of ethics, which can encompass a range of theoretical approaches to ethics. Particular ethical theories often narrow the sphere of ethics to one or two of these themes – or at least focus on one as the foundation or starting point of ethics. The dominant paradigm in contemporary writings on social work ethics tends to be based on principles of

5

conduct, including principles focusing on the promotion of rights to freedom of choice and action (deontological or Kantian approaches to ethics) and principles focusing on the greatest good of the greatest number of people (consequentialist or utilitarian approaches). However, there is a small but growing interest in ethical theories that focus on the character of the moral agent (virtue ethics) and the caring relationship between people (the ethics of care), both of which entail a vision of what counts as the good society or human flourishing. Radical or Marxist ethics would also start with a focus on the nature of human flourishing – seeing humans as essentially social beings.

'The ethics boom'

Davis (1999) used the term 'ethics boom' in the late 1990s to characterise the rapidly growing interest in the theme of ethics, including professional ethics. The 'boom' has continued apace – in social work as much as any other area. Indeed, the number of specialist textbooks on ethics in social work published in Europe and the English-speaking world is very rapidly growing (for example, Rouzel, 1997; Timmer, 1998; Lingås, 1999; Linzer, 1999; Reamer, 1999, 2006a; Beckett and Maynard, 2005; Bowles et al, 2006; Joseph and Fernandes, 2006; Charleton, 2007; Barsky, 2009; Clifford and Burke, 2009; Congress et al, 2009; Dolgoff et al, 2009; Gray and Webb, 2010; Banks, 2012; Banks and Nøhr, 2012). These texts generally cover ethical theories, codes of ethics, practice-related dilemmas and ethical decision-making. Principle-based theories of what counts as right and wrong are often invoked, although increasingly attention is being paid to character and relationship-based ethics (virtue ethics and the ethics of care).

There is also a growth of interest in codes of ethics published by professional associations and regulatory bodies. These usually provide statements about the core purpose of social work, the values and principles upon which it is based and some standards or rules to guide social workers' conduct. Many countries that did not have codes of ethics for social work developed them in the 1990s and 2000s, and in many instances, but not all, codes are getting longer each time they are revised, as the examples given in Table 1 show. The results of a survey of codes of ethics of professional associations for social work in 2005 (Banks, 2006, pp 74–102) suggest that the longer codes tend to be in the global North, in countries where social work is well established and where codes may be used to discipline social workers for misconduct.[3]

Codes of ethics tend to be action-focused (outlining ethical principles and rules of conduct), although, of course, they are framed in terms of the professional roles and relationships of social workers. The nature of the good society is not explicitly outlined in most codes of ethics, although a vision of certain features of a good society is implicit in the mission statements often included at the start of codes. Many of the national codes of ethics include the international definition of social work, which states that social work adheres to principles of human rights and social justice (IFSW and IASSW, 2004). Modern codes of ethics for social work tend to include few statements about the character of the social worker, although many do have one or two references to professional integrity and honesty – for example, the recently revised Australian code has professional integrity as one of the three core values (Australian Association of Social Workers, 2010). The expansion in size of codes of ethics is in the area of 'standards' or 'rules', which explicitly guide social workers' behaviour in a variety

Table 1: Some examples of lengthening professional codes of ethics

Code	Date 1980s/90s	Length	Date 2000s	Length
Australian Association of Social Workers	1989	7 pages	2010	33 pages (in a booklet of 54 pages)
National Association of Social Workers (USA)	1990	9 pages	2008	27 pages
Nederlandse Vereniging van Maatschappelijk Werkers (Netherlands)	1999	12 pages	2010	22 pages

of contexts. The proliferation of more prescriptive standards and rules in codes of ethics mirrors the trend in practice for more detailed and standardised systems of monitoring and assessment in social work, which is one of the features of what has been termed 'the new public management' (NPM).

The new public management

Before exploring the relationship between ethics in social work and NPM, I will first discuss the characteristics of NPM and the changing emphases over time, taking the UK as an example. In the UK, NPM has developed more quickly than in many other countries and has made a significant impact in the field of social work.

Markets, measurement and competition

The term 'new public management' covers a number of features of the organisational management of public services, which have varied over time and between countries. The term came into frequent use in the UK in the 1990s, when a marketised approach to public services began to take hold under Conservative government (1979–97). This involved the creation of actual or quasi-markets through separating purchasers and providers of services, introducing competition, measuring outputs and outcomes rather than inputs, working to targets, and the generation of procedures and regulations to maximise the effectiveness and efficiency of employees. Some of the key characteristics of NPM can be summarised as follows (Dunleavy and Hood, 1994; Clarke et al, 2000b):

- attention to outputs and performance rather than inputs;
- organisations being viewed as chains of low-trust relationships, linked by contracts or contractual-type processes;
- the separation of purchaser and provider or client and contractor roles within formerly integrated processes or organisations;
- breaking down large-scale organisations and using competition to enable 'exit' or 'choice' by service users;

- decentralisation of budgetary and personal authority to line managers.

These trends are exemplified by the following quotation from a senior social worker in the UK, whom I interviewed as part of a research project in 2001 (for further details, see Banks, 2004):

> "… overbearing procedures equate sometimes to, yes, it gives a checklist as to what processes should be followed every time and that can be quite useful in a number of settings, but, it also can be used as a stick to beat up social workers with if a particular procedure hasn't been followed to the letter…." (Social work team manager, child care)

Modernisation, outcomes and achievement

The focus on procedures, measurement and centrally defined targets intensified under the New Labour regime in the UK (1997–2010), although the language moved from 'new public management' to 'modernising' public services. The focus also shifted from cutting back on public welfare to a concern to achieve improved outcomes for people and communities in terms of social inclusion, educational attainment and neighbourhood regeneration, for example. This entailed policies that promoted 'joined up' government, interprofessional working and highly managed partnerships between politicians, professionals, communities and service users (Newman, 2000, 2005). These policies also reflected a concern with identifying and targeting the individuals and neighbourhoods regarded as most problematic, and focusing intense interventions and surveillance on these people and areas.

The following comment comes from a youth worker employed in an interprofessional youth offending team (YOT) (for more details of this case, see Banks, 2009). He was working with young people who had committed a first criminal offence and who had been given a 'final warning'. He was supposed to work with them for 12 weeks, but he was spending longer. This was problematic for his manager because the interventions were being monitored nationally, and by not closing cases he was compromising the success rate of his team:

> "So the intervention package is supposed to be for 12 weeks. I'm in very big trouble at the YOT, because I've got cases that are nearly a year old now. And I keep trying to explain, this is about *the youth work dilemma* … I'm about the process of trying to get this young person from here to somewhere. Going in rattling at them for 12 weeks is going just to produce nothing, because when I shut the case and walk away in 12 weeks' time, they will … get themselves in trouble…."

Austerity, economy and efficiency

Following the economic crisis in 2008, and the election of a new Conservative-led Coalition Government in 2010, a major programme of public sector cuts is being implemented in the UK, with many non-statutory welfare services being closed by local authorities, or taken over by third sector (non-governmental) organisations or private organisations. Although one of the themes of this Coalition Government is the removal of bureaucracy and centralised targets, the cuts in local government funding mean that for public services to survive in local authorities, they need to demonstrate efficiency and effectiveness. And in the case of those welfare services and facilities that are contracted out or sold off to third sector and private organisations, the demand for performance measures, including value for money and social return on investment, is as important as ever. So the requirement to be able to provide evidence of performance outputs and outcomes remains and looks set to intensify, although some of the centrally imposed targets, systems of regulation, audit and inspection, and the management posts required to implement these systems, may have disappeared.

In the UK there is evidence of a turn against excessively procedure-driven practice in public welfare services, especially in the field of child protection where this approach has been very dominant. For example, a major review was conducted by Professor Eileen Munro, an academic from the London School of Economics and Political Science, during 2010–11. At the start of the first report, Munro comments:

> A dominant theme in the criticisms of current practice is the skew in priorities that has developed between the demands of the management and inspection processes and professionals' ability to exercise their professional judgment and act in the best interests of the child. This has led to an over-standardised system that cannot respond adequately to the varied range of children's needs.
>
> … For some, following rules and being compliant can appear less risky than carrying the personal responsibility for exercising judgment. (Munro, 2011, pp 5–6)

Clear evidence for Munro's comments can be found in the findings of a well-publicised research project that graphically exposed the ineffectiveness and demoralising effect on social workers of the implementation of a national computerised system for micro-managing and recording child care social work (White et al, 2010).

There was also an English government-sponsored 'Social Work Task Force' that reviewed the state of social work during 2009–2010, succeeded by a 'Social Work Reform Board', with the aim of improving effectiveness and increasing the professional credibility and status of social work. Proposed reforms include new national standards of practice, continuing education and professional development, supervision, changes to professional education and the introduction of a national College of Social Work – a high-profile professional body (Department for Education, 2010). It is noteworthy that the role of social workers frequently tends to be described in the report of the Reform Board as 'support', and the emphasis is on 'safe' practice, professionalism, standards and status. A retreat to a position where the aspiration of social work is to become and be regarded as safe and professional is, of course, not surprising in a government-sponsored report written during a period of economic crisis and under a Conservative-dominated government.

How these reviews will change social work practice remains to be seen, especially in times of economic austerity. However, it is certainly the case in the UK that the public service cuts are giving added weight to demands for reductions in bureaucracy, national target-setting, audit and inspection. In 2010, the newly elected Coalition Government abandoned proposals for an ambitious national database for recording details of all children and young people, showing which agencies were working with them (Barr, 2010). Similarly in 2011, a complex new national system for vetting all volunteers working with children and other vulnerable people was significantly scaled back (Department for Education et al, 2011). So the time is certainly right for those practitioners and academics who have been advocating a rolling-back of state bureaucracy, but unfortunately it is also being accompanied by a drastic reduction in state-sponsored welfare services for the poorest sections of society.

The various components of 'NPM' have shifted over time, and are still shifting. Some commentators have suggested that we are now in an era of post-NPM or digital governance (Dunleavy et al, 2006; Levy, 2010) as certain features of NPM, such as centralised targets and auditing, are diminishing. Yet many of the trends identified as part of NPM (measurement, value for money, privatisation) are still prevailing and indeed intensifying. Hence I will use this term to refer to continuing trends towards marketisation, the measurement of outcomes of welfare services and the regulation of welfare professionals. However, as time goes by in the UK and elsewhere, this concept may need further revision in the context of the 'new public austerity' ('NPA').[4]

Ethics and the new public management

I will now explore two ways of looking at the relationship between ethics and the new public management in social work. The first sees the growth of interest in ethics as a reaction against the worst excesses of NPM; while the second sees the growth of interest in ethics as part of the trend towards NPM approaches.

The growth of interest in ethics as progressive and critical of NPM

As suggested earlier, concern with ethics can be regarded as an important counter-balance to the tendency in NPM to focus on technical aspects of social work practice – a counter-balance to seeing social workers as technicians or bureaucrats, service users as targets or consumers, and social work as instrumental in maintaining fundamental social inequalities. This entails a view of ethics as being about autonomous (free) agents choosing right actions based not just on ethical principles and rules, but also on qualities of character and relationships of care, with an emphasis on the needs and rights of actual and potential service users.

1. *Reclaiming professional autonomy.* Ethics has a focus on human agency – on moral agents making considered choices and taking right actions in a social context. In social work, this relates to social workers' professional autonomy and discretion in making judgements and decisions in accordance with their professional knowledge, experience and the values of social work. Social workers are not mere technicians or bureaucrats following rules. They have professional expertise and are committed to ethical practice. Social workers have the right, power and duty to promote what they regard as good and ethical practice and to challenge and resist inhumane, degrading and unjust practices and policies.
2. *Asserting the needs and claiming the rights of service users.* Ethics in social work is about working with service users to identify their needs and promoting and respecting the rights of service users to make their own decisions and/or to work in partnership with social workers. Core ethical values in social work include respecting the dignity of service users and respecting their rights and choices, as opposed to viewing them as problems to be solved, victims to be blamed, targets to be reached or consumers to be satisfied.

13

3. *Reasserting the social justice mission of social work – bringing the political to the heart of ethics.* Social justice is a core ethical value at the heart of social work. This includes a commitment to distributing welfare services fairly in accordance with need; the recognition of diversity and difference (eg in terms of gender, ethnicity or ability); and challenging oppressive power structures. It also entails questioning the power and interests of governments, public service employers, private corporations and social workers themselves that cause them to ignore or accept inequalities and oppression. These values may sometimes be branded as 'political', but I would see them as 'ethico-political'.

4. *Reconfiguring professional ethics – bringing the personal back into social work ethics.* Ethics is about the person (moral agent) and interpersonal relationships, as well as actions and abstract principles. Much of the recent literature on social work ethics includes reference to virtue ethics and the ethics of care. Some theorists argue for a reframing of professional ethics to focus on the moral qualities, commitments and motivations of social workers, or on the nature of the caring relationship between worker and service users. These approaches highlight the importance of empathy, compassion and care, and build on the traditional concern of social work with valuing each individual person in the context of their particular lives, hopes and aspirations.

The growth of interest in ethics as regressive and compliant with NPM

There is an alternative interpretation of the growth of interest in ethics, which sees this as part of (and reinforcing) the same trends as NPM. Clearly this is based on a different view of what 'ethics' is – associating ethics with regulation and conformity of professional social workers (rather than autonomy), social responsibilities of social workers and service users, and the individualising of social problems through a focus on individual dilemmas.

1. *Developing more regulatory codes of ethics.* Professional ethics is often strongly associated with codes of ethics. As already noted, codes of ethics are getting longer and offering more detailed guidance about what to do in particular circumstances. They are sometimes – but not always – used for disciplinary purposes (in cases of misconduct by social workers). This can be seen as a response to the low public esteem in which social workers are held and as a way of attempting to ensure social workers do not bring the profession into disrepute. It also suggests that social workers need guidance in relation to small details of their work and hence raises doubts about the degree to which they can and should exercise professional discretion. The responsibilities or standards listed in the professional codes of ethics are sometimes presented in the introductions to the codes as 'guidance' (NASW, 2008). However, the way they are framed ('social workers should …') suggests a strong expectation that these guiding standards should be followed and would be taken into account in any disciplinary proceedings against social workers.

2. *Highlighting the responsibilities of social workers and service users ('responsibilisation').* Ethics, with its focus on agency and choice, can result in drawing attention to the responsibilities of individual social workers for making good or bad decisions and taking right or wrong actions and the responsibilities of service users for the causes of social problems. This links to the tendency to blame individual social workers, rather than, or as well as, their employing institutions or government, if there is a bad outcome of a particular case, or if the quality of service is poor. The focus on the individual service user or family can also make it easier to locate blame and responsibility for the causes of problems with individuals rather than with structural inequalities.

3. *Placing the focus of attention on the relationship between the individual social worker and service user or family.* The way ethical issues are framed can serve to focus social workers' attention at the level of the individual service user and family, and away from offering critiques of social policy and taking political action. This occurs through a discourse that highlights ethical issues as being about individual

social workers making decisions in difficult circumstances, divorced from the broader policy or political context. A significant feature of many ethics textbooks is discussion of ethical dilemmas based on short, decontextualised cases. At the end of the case, a question is asked about what the social worker should do in this case – for example, break or preserve confidentiality; recommend a child is removed from their parents, or left with the family. This results in a framing of ethical issues as dilemmas for individuals.

4. *De-personalising and de-politicising of ethics.* The growing trend to link ethics with regulation, conformity to pre-defined standards and contract-type relationships is resulting in a de-personalised ethics. It leads to a model of the ethical relationship as one of a contract between several parties (specified and agreed in advance, when each follows the rules) rather than one based on mutual trust. If the emphasis is on conformity to externally defined standards and rules, which are to be applied in a standard way in every case, this results in an ethics that focuses on impartiality, objectivity and impersonal treatment. This leads to a focus on equity at the expense of empathy, achieving good economic outcomes for society (effectiveness and efficiency) at the expense of meeting the needs of oppressed and impoverished individual people and groups (equality). It encourages a narrow vision of the role of social work divorced from people with personalities and from political debates about what counts as fairness or equality.

Contradictory trends

This discussion suggests that there may be a variety of different and contradictory reasons for the growing interest in ethics at the present time; and the 'ethics boom' may have a variety of different and contradictory effects. For example, the focus of ethics on individual moral agency can be positive in that it encourages social workers to see themselves as moral agents who can and should resist unjust and inhumane practices. Yet this inevitably also places the burden of responsibility on them when things go wrong. Social workers need to see themselves as a part of collective struggles to achieve a just society. This entails a commitment to taking power and responsibility where they can in order to achieve good and just outcomes for or with service users, and also to challenge the general public, media and politicians when social workers are specifically blamed for a bad outcome (the death of a child, the injury of an older person). Social workers also need to be aware that excessive concern with professional autonomy can result in parentalism on the part of social workers (meaning that the social worker is the expert who knows what is best or right) – marginalising or ignoring the views of service users. Similarly, a concern with personal relationships is positive in that it mitigates against treating people as cases, consumers or numbers. Yet excessive concern with the individual person and the social worker–service user relationship can lead to the ignoring of the bigger picture – the structural and societal problems. Social workers have to acknowledge and work with these contradictions, which are part of what constitutes social work and are held in a dialectical tension – a complex interplay between opposites (Mullaly, 1997, pp 127–31).

This discussion clearly shows how the ethics agenda can be co-opted into the service of NPM. It also gives us some pointers as to how features of the traditional model of professional ethics (particularly the tendency to focus on the professional autonomy of the social worker and the individual relationship between the service user and the social worker) may need to be modified or strengthened to resist this co-option. This is especially important given that NPM has developed alongside de-professionalising trends (suspicion of professionals as elitist and excessively powerful), a concern with measuring and managing risk, and a severe crisis of welfare-capitalism.

Reclaiming and reframing ethics in social work

I will end this article with some suggestions for reclaiming a progressive and radical ethics for social work. It is important to extend the topic of ethics beyond the focus on professional codes of conduct and the individual moral agent acting rationally on the basis of ethical principles

—

17

and rules. Whilst ethics in social work certainly covers matters of professional responsibility, accountability and discretion, the subject matter of ethics cannot be divorced from personal commitments and values or from the wider political and social context in which it takes place.

Ethics as personal and political: towards a situated ethics of social justice

- *Situated ethics* – it is important to see ethical issues as embedded in everyday practice and in people's lives. Ethics is not just about dilemmas and making difficult decisions about rights and resources by rational deduction from abstract principles. All facets of life have ethical dimensions. Ethical being and ethical action require sensitivity to the particularities of situations and human relationships, and encompass emotion (empathy, care and compassion) as well as reason. One example of a situated approach to ethics relevant to social work is the ethics of care, which takes human relationships as its starting point.
- *Politicised ethics* – if we regard social work as a social movement as much as a profession or job, then we need to relate social work ethics explicitly to movements that promote practice that is variously categorised as anti-oppressive, critical, structural and radical. In the process of reclaiming the social work profession as an occupational group in alliance/struggle alongside service users, people in poverty and victims of injustice, social workers need to keep hold of a radical account of social justice, a sense of solidarity and willingness to speak out and take action.

One approach to ethics that encompasses both these features is what the American feminist philosopher Joan Tronto (1993, 2010) terms a *political ethics of care*, which focuses on human relationships in the context of structures of power and oppression. Such an approach has been taken forward very compellingly by the Dutch political theorist Selma Sevenhuijsen (1998) and is beginning to be discussed in some of the literature for the social professions in Holland (Lohman & Raaf, 2001, quoted in Philippart, 2012; Wilken, 2010) and other countries (Clifford and Burke, 2009). This is very useful for theorising the relationships that are at the heart of social work in both personal and political terms. It can respond to accusations laid against early versions of radical (particularly Marxist) approaches to social work in the 1970s that they adopted utilitarian value perspectives, using service users for political ends.

However, I have chosen to speak instead of a *situated ethics of social justice* rather than a *political ethics of care*. In practice this may be hardly distinguishable from a political ethics of care. However, at a conceptual level it takes social justice as its starting point, qualified by the term 'situated', rather than starting with 'care', qualified by 'political'. It is an attempt to develop further an ethics for 'the new radical social work' that is being promoted through the Social Work Action Network (SWAN) and the literature that is emerging from some of its activists (for example, Ferguson, 2008; Ferguson and Woodward, 2009; Lavalette, 2011). The list below can be regarded as a tentative starting point for developing the SWAN (2004) manifesto.

Preliminary values for a situated ethics of social justice in social work

1. *Radical social justice.* Social workers need to take seriously the social justice agenda contained within international and other definitions and descriptions of social work as being about working for equality of outcomes and challenging unjust policies and practices. We need to be alert to the variety of formulations of social justice (such as the more liberal reformist focus on equal opportunities) and hold onto a conception that embraces a call to challenge the five faces of oppression as identified by Iris Marion Young (1990, p 41): exploitation, marginalisation, powerlessness, cultural imperialism and violence.

2. *Empathic solidarity.* Part of the role of social workers is to situate themselves in relation to the hopes, fears, pains and pleasures of other people, specifically service users. Empathy on its own, however,

---

is not enough. It needs to lead to the development of a sense of solidarity and commitment to collective action for social change. This empathic solidarity requires abilities of critical analysis and an aspirational or hopeful attitude – this involves seeing the bigger picture, questioning received ideas and seeing the possibility for another kind of world.

3. *Relational autonomy.* It is important that social workers claim power as moral agents to work for progressive micro-level and macro-level social change. However, we need to reframe individual professional autonomy as 'relational autonomy'. This involves recognising that autonomy is both defined and pursued in a social context (including structures of oppression) and this influences the opportunities an individual has to develop and exercise autonomy (McLeod and Sherwin, 2000). In social work the exercise of professional autonomy is also based on 'power with' others, including service users.

4. *Collective responsibility for resistance.* Social workers should take responsibility for good and just practice, and for resisting bad and unjust practice and policies. This is the counterpart to claiming autonomy. But in seeing their autonomy as relational (that is, in the context of oppressive and constraining structures and institutions), it is important that they resist the responsibilisation of social workers, service users and people in poverty. This means that social workers should actively resist, with service users and other allies, the placing of responsibility for the causes and solutions of social problems with individuals, families and communities. This responsibility is shared with all fellow citizens and the responsibility for taking action is also collective as well as individual. This could also be termed 'relational responsibility'.

5. *Moral courage.* Moral courage is a quality or disposition to act in situations where such actions are difficult, uncomfortable or fear-inducing. Courage is one of the moral qualities or virtues that is vital for social work and is further elaborated in Banks and Gallagher (2009, pp 72–95), along with several other important virtues in professional life. Many aspects of social work require moral courage – to knock on the door of the house of a family whose child is

under threat of removal or to challenge a racist comment by a service user. Moral courage is also required to speak out about inadequate resources and policies that impact disproportionately on people who are in need or difficulty. The kind of moral courage required in such contexts is buttressed if based on a sense of collective responsibility and solidarity.

6. *Working in and with complexity and contradictions.* In social work, complexity, uncertainty, ambivalence and contradictions need to be acknowledged and used, along with the recognition that ethics is not about simple dilemmas, that is choices between two courses of action. Ethical being and action require hard work on the part of social workers – a process of constantly negotiating and working out what roles to take, questioning what they are doing and why, and being alert to the dominance of the managerialist and neoliberal agendas. It entails working in the spaces between the contradictions of care and control, prevention and enforcement, empathy and equity. Ethics is definitely not about simply following rules – it is about questioning and challenging, feeling and acting.

These values are a mixture of principles of action and moral qualities, premised on a relational worldview that emphasises the importance of solidarity and collective action. This list is a preliminary statement, which is not designed to replace existing sets of values articulated in codes of ethics. Indeed, these values are not new – they are old values that need to be constantly restated and reworked in order to remind us of their importance and to reclaim them from dilution or co-option by NPM or other negative trends in society. Versions of these values can be found in the academic literature, the international statement on ethics in social work and many national codes of ethics and other literature. But in the midst of a crowd of other exhortations and injunctions in codes of ethics of 30–50 pages, their significance can be lost, or they can be regarded as another example of social work's radical rhetoric that means little in practice, or is untranslatable into practice. However, it is up to us to ensure that these values can be translated into practice and to show how this can be, and is being, done, by many social workers around the world.

This 'progressive model' of a situated ethics of social justice would see ethics as essential to justifying and enabling resistance in professional life – whether that resistance be the 'quiet challenges' of the youth worker in the youth offending team refusing to close his cases after 12 weeks, or the more noisy challenges that accompany a campaign to save a youth service, to challenge laws on asylum seekers' rights or to expose the inequities of high interest loans to people in poverty.

Concluding comments

This article has argued that 'reclaiming the ethical' is not only about reasserting a set of progressive values for social work, but also about engaging in critical analysis of how the domain of 'the ethical' is framed. A co-option of 'ethics' to refer to the creation and following of rules of good conduct not only undermines fundamental features of ethics – traditionally conceived as involving individual moral agents engaging in moral struggles and grappling with dilemmas. It also allows the topic of ethics to be co-opted to managerialist and neoliberal agendas as a way of disciplining social workers and service users and encouraging conformity, compliance, blame and responsibility in a time of increasing poverty and inequality.

In these times of growing local and global protests and social movements – against authoritarian regimes, the inequities of the financial markets, the restructuring of welfare regimes or demanding action on climate change – the 'ethical' is emerging more forcefully as part of the radical project. As Paulo Freire commented in the last letter in his posthumously published collection *The Pedagogy of Indignation*:

> If we do indeed wish to overcome the disequilibrium between North and South, between power and fragility, between strong economies and weak economies, we cannot afford to be without ethics, but obviously not the ethics of the market. (Freire, 2004, p 117)

—

Notes

[1] This lead essay draws on an article published in 2011 in the *Journal of Social Intervention: Theory and Practice*, vol 20, no 2, pp 5–23, under the title of 'Ethics in an age of austerity: social work and the evolving new public management'. I am grateful to the journal for permission to use the material from that article, which was based on a lecture at University of Applied Sciences Utrecht and a presentation given at a joint Japan–UK seminar in Tokyo in March 2011, funded by the Economic and Social Research Council and the Japanese Society for the Promotion of Science.

[2] Whilst some theorists distinguish between 'ethics' and 'morality', these terms are frequently used interchangeably (one derives from Greek and the other from Latin, both relating to habits or customs). In the literature quoted here no clear distinction is made. However, a common distinction (see Banks, 2012, pp 6-7) is between 'morality' as a set of externally imposed universal values, absolute and imperative, to which individuals must relate themselves and 'ethics' as constructed norms of internal consistency. Bouquet (1999, p 27) suggests that common usage is now substituting 'ethics' for 'morality', as 'morality' has become discredited through being confused with 'moralising' (making absolute judgements on matters of right and wrong, often with a superior air). This is precisely the sense in which Marx is using the term 'morality', which Eagleton then goes on to characterise as 'moralism'(the practice of moralising).

[3] In the UK the role of registering and disciplining professionally qualified social workers was taken on by statutory regulatory bodies (one for each of the four countries of the UK from the mid-2000s). These bodies developed their own codes of practice, which are used in misconduct hearings (eg Scottish Social Services Council, 2009), although social work in England was absorbed within what is now known as the Health Professions Council in 2012.

[4] While I have invented the term 'new public austerity', the term 'new austerity' is in common usage.

A roadmap for social work ethics: reflections and a proposal

Frederic G. Reamer

Confucius is known to have said: 'By three methods we may learn wisdom: First, by reflection, which is noblest; second, by imitation, which is easiest; and third by experience, which is the bitterest.'

I have been deeply privileged to participate, over many years, in the rich international dialogue concerning the nature and status of social work ethics. I dare say that our efforts have paid off; the evolution of our grasp of ethical issues and challenges counts as one of the most remarkable developments in the profession's history. Consistent with Confucius's claim, our gains are the product of disciplined reflection informed by sometimes painful experience.

Sarah Banks wisely observes that approaches to social work ethics are a function of political and economic climate and ideology; ambitious contemporary efforts to market social work, use empirical metrics to assess outcomes, promote competition among private sector providers, and achieve economic efficiencies have seriously compromised social workers' commitment to our world's most vulnerable, least advantaged citizens. Indeed, there is some real risk that ethical standards in social work are being co-opted and used to enhance regulation of practitioners' conduct rather than promote the profession's broader aims. Banks is right to assert that current trends in social work ethics demand constructively critical analysis and reflection. Her principal thesis – that 'it is important to extend the topic of ethics beyond the focus on professional codes of conduct and the individual moral agent acting rationally on the basis of ethical principles and rules' – is spot on.

The devil, however, is in the detail. Reasonable minds may differ regarding the very best ways to forge that path. I would like to share my own views on the matter.

The evolution of social work ethics

Before we focus on essential questions concerning the current status and future of social work ethics, it is important to reflect on the road we have taken to the present. Although past is not always prologue, often it is, at least in some important respects.

Recognising that the theme of values and ethics has endured throughout the profession's history, social workers' conceptions of what these terms mean have changed over time. The evolution of social work values and ethics has had several key stages: the *morality period*, *values period*, *ethical theory and decision-making period*, and *ethical standards and risk management period*. The morality period began in the late 19th century, when social work was formally inaugurated as a profession. During this period social work was much more concerned about the morality of the client than about the morality or ethics of the profession or its practitioners.

Concern about the morality of the client receded somewhat during the next several decades of the profession's life – the values period – as practitioners engaged in earnest attempts to establish and polish their intervention strategies and techniques, training programmes, and schools of thought. After a half century of development, the social work profession was moving into a phase characterised by efforts to develop consensus about the profession's core values (Pumphrey, 1959; Emmet, 1962; Younghusband, 1967; Levy, 1973; Timms, 1983).

In the late 1970s the profession underwent another significant transition as it moved into the ethical theory and decision-making period. During this period there was a dramatic surge of interest among social workers (and many other professionals, for example, physicians, nurses, journalists, engineers, business professionals and lawyers) in the

---

broad subject of applied and professional ethics (also known as practical ethics); this included ambitious attempts to apply ethical theories (especially deontology and teleology or consequentialism) to ethical dilemmas and develop conceptually based decision-making protocols (Reamer, 1993, 2013; Beckett and Maynard, 2005; Banks, 2012).

The most recent stage in the development of social work ethics – the ethical standards and risk management period – reflects the dramatic maturation of social workers' understanding of ethical issues. This stage is characterised mainly by the significant expansion of ethical standards to guide practitioners' conduct and by increased knowledge concerning professional negligence and liability (Barker and Branson, 2000; Barsky, 2009; Houston-Vega et al, 1997; Reamer, 2003, 2006a).

Banks' keen observations suggest that social work may be embarking – or, more precisely, ought to embark – on yet another significant phase, what we might call the post-modern phase. Consistent with this perspective, which is characterised by raising critical questions about long-standing ideological assumptions that may be a function of political and economic power, Banks encourages social workers to think hard about prevailing views of social work ethics. Based on her claims concerning the possible misuse or co-option of social work ethics to further the interests of powerful regulators and administrators who serve the new public management, Banks smartly urges social workers to embrace 'situated' ethics, which favours context over formulaic, impersonal, ethical decision-making algorithms; values the influence of trust, empathy and relationship in the navigation of ethical issues; and focuses on broad public issues in addition to individuals' private troubles.

The essence of contemporary social work ethics

In important respects, the evolution of social work ethics reflects broader, long-standing tensions in social work. Banks is right to say that there is real risk that current ethical standards and codes of conduct may lead social workers to focus on narrow, case-related circumstances rather than broad, fundamental questions of social justice

27

that involve challenging oppressive, exploitative and discriminatory practices and institutions (Lundy, 2004). Preoccupation with case-based moral outcomes and compliance with ethical standards runs the risk of diverting social workers from the broader moral purposes and mission of the profession (Gil, 1998). This is reminiscent of the early 20th-century debate about the relationship between 'case' and 'cause' in social work (Reeser and Epstein, 1990). Students of social work history know that one of the profession's hallmarks – since the time of Jane Addams and Mary Richmond – has been the integration of 'case' (helping individual clients address and cope with life's challenges) and 'cause' (engaging in social action, advocacy and reform efforts).

In principle, social work has never been an 'either/or' profession, focusing exclusively on clinical or reform efforts. Indeed, one of social work's most cherished attributes is its simultaneous commitment to individual well-being and broader social concerns. Ideally, social workers will acknowledge the wisdom of Banks' exhortations to challenge immoral, self-serving social institutions and structures without abandoning their concern about case-based ethics they encounter in their 'retail' work with individuals, couples, families and small groups. We should not interpret Banks' assertions to mean that social workers must choose between focusing on post-modern questions about the nature of social work ethics and engaging in practical – and compelling – ethical judgements. Both are essential elements of today's social work practice.

So where does this leave us? Banks has pushed the social work ethics envelope and suggested new borders for social work's moral enterprise. In my view, we should fold Banks' sensible mandate into our evolving understanding of what we mean by social work ethics without abandoning what have become core components of the phenomenon. Towards this end, I propose that social work ethics for today's practitioners incorporate five key elements.

1. *The value base of the social work profession.* Social workers must continue to examine their beliefs about core values that have served as the profession's ballast. Although many values – such as

—

the dignity, uniqueness and worth of the person, self-determination, autonomy, respect, justice, equality, fairness and individuation – have endured in the profession since the late 19th century, there have been significant changes over time. Today's social workers must focus on emerging global issues concerning allocation of limited social resources and novel human rights concerns, for example regarding sexual exploitation of teens by human traffickers and discrimination against immigrants and people who are gay, lesbian and transgender.

2. *Ethical dilemmas in social work.* Social work will always produce challenging ethical dilemmas where practitioners' duties and obligations clash. Clinical social workers face difficult judgements about the limits of clients' right to confidentiality and self-determination. Social work managers face difficult ethical choices about compliance with unjust laws and allocating limited resources. Social work organisers face dilemmas concerning the morality of civil disobedience in their work with community groups that object to draconian government policies and regulations. Social workers who serve in policy and advocacy positions struggle with hard choices concerning the role of government and the private sector in efforts to meet the needs of vulnerable people. As social work evolves, social workers must continue to identify ethical dilemmas that have profound implications for clients' lives.

3. *Ethical decision making in social work.* Since the early 1980s social workers have grown to appreciate ethicists' efforts to construct sound, reasonable and practical ethical decision-making protocols and frameworks. Banks is right to raise concerns about the possibility that such guidelines will become formulaic algorithms that compromise social workers' decision-making autonomy and steer attention away from efforts to promote trust, empathic solidarity, character, virtue, integrity and the capacity to engage in meaningful professional relationships. That said, social workers will continue to need well-constructed, practical decision-making guides.

4. *Ethical standards and risk management.* Especially since the early 1990s social workers have spent considerable effort refining and expanding ethical standards in an effort to protect clients, themselves and their

—

employers. Yes, there is a risk that this ethical apparatus will distract social workers from concern about broad social justice issues. Yet, in my experience, the expansion of ethical standards – while not without costs – has not led the profession down a slippery slope that has undermined its principal purpose. Nonetheless, Banks is right to worry; indeed, there is some risk that concern about compliance with formal ethical standards will compromise social workers' autonomy and play into the sometimes not-so-noble purposes of the power elite and become a substitute for concern about social justice. Our task is to strike the right balance as we seek to refine the profession's ethical standards.

5. *Post-modern questions about the moral purposes of the profession.* Banks has sent out a critically important message: as social work seeks its place in contemporary society, practitioners must raise constructively critical questions about whether and how the power elite lead social workers to subvert the profession's honourable moral mission, namely, to meet the needs of our world's most vulnerable citizens (Ferguson, 2008). We must ensure that this exhortation continues to ring in our ears.

To ensure that contemporary ethics provides the moral fuel for social work's mission, we must, as Confucius would say, engage in earnest reflection, especially about the noble purposes of the profession. And as we reflect on the essence of social work ethics, we must acknowledge that motives matter. A truly enlightened view of social work ethics elevates moral mission above self-interest and the interests of the power elite. After all, this is what it means to be an ethical social worker.

Contextualising the 'ethics boom'

Stephen Cowden

> We have found no way to replace capitalism as an effective
> mode of production, and yet that capitalist society as it actually
> functions violates all conceptions of a rational moral order.
> (Alistair MacIntyre, 1979, cited in Blackledge, 2012, p 1)

Sarah Banks has, in the lead article, clearly and concisely set out
the challenges facing social work, which are a consequence of the
dominance of new public management (NPM) in public services in
the UK. My response is concerned with trying to contextualise this
and spell out the challenges further, which may be in some senses
more profound than Sarah suggests in terms of defending social work
as an ethical enterprise.

Sarah outlines the way NPM originated under the Conservatives
in the 1990s, but also notes the way that this was hugely expanded
under New Labour. The result of this was that NPM was given a
legitimacy it never could have had when it was primarily identified
with a Thatcherite politics. In a sense the New Labour 'modernisation'
project, rather than representing a return to, or even a modernisation
of, the principles of the welfare state, was a continuation of a free
market, neoliberal 'common sense', albeit with greater state funding.
Stuart Hall has recently made the point that 'New Labour came closer
to institutionalising neo-liberalism as a social and political form than
Thatcher did', particularly as Tony Blair's language found ways making
these ideas acceptable 'to Labour voters as well' (Derbyshire, 2012).

Sarah's discussion includes the example of the way agencies were
expected to target scarce resources to those who 'need them most'. The
use of this approach by New Labour effectively shifted the discourse

of welfare away from a universalist conception, one of the primary achievements of the post-war welfare state, and thus opened the way to a much more punitive and controlling conception of welfare. These practices have already had a massive impact on social work practice, particularly in the area of children and families, which is now hugely stigmatised, and of course this process has been aided and abetted by the reactionary Murdoch press. (Although many of those who waged war against social work are now potentially facing prison sentences for corruption and dishonesty, the social work profession is unlikely to receive an apology.) It has been through processes such as this that social work's social justice and humanitarian mission has been undermined, from both within and without.

The other key aspects of NPM were the extensive use of audit and performance targets, and many commentators, including Jordan (2006, 2010) and Clarke et al (2000b) have noted, these changes sought to circumscribe professional discretion, shifting power away from frontline workers towards managers. The third achievement of New Labour was to advance the argument that there was no good reason, other than backward-looking socialist dogmatism, for services to be publicly owned; what was important was 'what works'. Ownership did not matter – all that mattered was the effectiveness of the service.

It is these developments which form the context to the 'ethics boom' that Sarah refers to, which was of a piece with the New Labour modernisation agenda. On one hand it worked as a legitimation strategy; though many areas of social care were now in private hands, they were still expected to function 'ethically'. Sarah notes that this expansion of codes of ethics also represented a means of regulating professionals themselves. It is in this context that we have to understand the focus on 'social work values' among social workers seeking to defend social work's social justice mission, demonstrated, for example, by the huge attendance at the Nottingham conference in March 2006 (the proceedings of which were subsequently published as Barnard et al, 2008). Sarah, who was one of the main speakers at this event, concludes her discussion by setting out what she sees as the key issues with which those concerned with the ongoing defence of social work as a progressive institution need to be concerned. While I entirely in agreement with the principles she puts forward here, I want to suggest that what is missing is a lack of attention to organisational structures, ownership and fundamental questions of accountability.

This brings me to the quote with which I began this response. I want to argue that ongoing developments have pointed to the delusional nature of the New Labour third way arguments – questions of ownership are really important as they go to the heart of questions of accountability and thereby of ethics. We need once again to start talking about 'capitalism' and the impact that it has on communities where the workers in a particular area are cast off because corporations are able to make greater profits elsewhere. In this sense I am not convinced that the progressive focus on 'anti-oppressive practice' is at all adequate in terms of what we face, and this has become even more the case following the change of government in the UK in 2010, heralding an even more regressive agenda. Here the prize is to entirely replace the concept of welfare entitlements as 'rights' with a consumerist discourse about a 'good service', with all of these services, including social work itself, run as private services. In this sense it is now clear that NPM was not the end game, but rather yet another stage in the ongoing erosion of a sense of public space and the 'social', which is central to neoliberal social policy. As I have argued with others elsewhere (Cowden and Singh, 2007; Pullen-Sansfacon and Cowden, 2012), a key difficulty in resisting this is the fact that much of the language through which the progressive dimensions within social work were expressed has itself been colonised by neoliberal discourse to serve entirely different ends. The term 'empowerment', once a key theme in giving a voice to those who were excluded and marginalised, has now come to mean that we all have to accept 'personal responsibility' for making the best choices for our and our families health, welfare and education. As Karen Baistow has noted:

> ... not being in control of your everyday living arrangements,
> your time, your diet, your body, your health, your children,

—

suggests that there is something seriously wrong with your ethical constitution. (Baistow, 1994, p 37)

A term which was championed by radicals and was once the bête noire of conservatives has now become part of the discourse through which the poorest and most marginalised sections of the community are once again pathologised and controlled. This capture of formerly progressive language and concepts has had the effect of disorienting many within the profession who genuinely want to practise anti-oppressively, at the same time as a new generation has entered the profession who have internalised these expectations of themselves and service users far less critically.

The second reason for bringing 'capitalism' back into our vocabulary is that private ownership means that banks and financiers are now making key decisions about how social care organisations operate on day-to-day basis. The very organisations that should have been reined in after their collapse in 2008, not to mention demonstrations of ongoing corruption, are being given ever more power over our social institutions. This was clearly demonstrated by the collapse of Southern Cross care homes in June 2011, which occurred after the private equity firm Blackstone separated out the property value of the homes from their actual running costs. This allowed company directors and shareholders to enrich themselves as the value of the company multiplied to four times its original value, but this financial engineering caused its collapse three years later, leaving 31,000 older people and 44,000 care staff as pawns in the machinations of stock market. What meaning does any code of ethics have in a situation like this?

Similar dynamics were demonstrated in another scandal which broke around the same time when appalling abuse at the Winterbourne View care home was exposed in May 2011 by the BBC Panorama programme. This home was run by the Castlebeck, a private care organisation, and following its exposure, politicians were very quick to assert that the problems were not in any way related to private ownership as such. While there have always been abuses of power in institutions for vulnerable people, the key point is that allowing for-profit operators and financiers to take over this area of care does not in any sense reduce that possibility, and, indeed, in an era where regulation of these institutions is characterised as the 'dead hand' of the state versus the thrusting entrepreneurialism of the private sector, abuse is in fact made more likely. In addition the BBC revealed that numerous care staff had contacted the Care Quality Commission to report abuse over several years, but no action had been taken; and this points to the essentially collusive arrangement that exists between private care operators and their so-called regulators.

Social work, like all those remaining progressive centres within the welfare state, faces a very troubled future, but one of the things we must take heart from is that it is precisely in a moment like this when the crisis is so serious, that genuinely new forces can emerge. I would conclude by pointing to the way we need to become part of this. The first thing we need is organisation: we need our trade unions, our professional organisations, our issue-based networks, our activist groups, and we should be as involved as we can be in these, as without organisation we are finished. Secondly we need analysis: we need to educate ourselves as to what neoliberalism is, how it has managed to be as successful as it has, but we also need to understand how important its current crisis is, and why it is so vital that we begin to resist. David McNally's excellent book *Global slump* (2010) is a really good place to start in terms of understanding this. Finally none of this is going to be easy. To raise these questions is to be cast immediately as difficult, backward, awkward. It is in this sense that analysis, which gives us the thinking tools to see through the forest of obfuscation and grasp what is really going on, is linked with organisation, which allows us to overcome our isolation and find our voices. And finally to achieve all of this, we must have moral courage. Sarah defines this as 'a quality or disposition to act in situations where such actions are difficult, uncomfortable or fear-inducing'. If we are to going to take on the might of neoliberal 'common sense', we are going to need a load of that as well.

Reframing social work ethics through a political ethic of care and social justice lens

Vivienne Bozalek

Sarah Banks' article on reclaiming social work ethics and challenging the new public management has strong resonance for me. I share many of her perceptions of our current situation, what is important for a radical ethics, and how social justice positions which encompass difference and the political ethics of care positions may be combined to form a critical situated and political ethics for social workers.

In this response I give my interpretation of the major arguments about ethics that Sarah Banks is proposing for the social work community, and I indicate where I support her positions and where I disagree. Since I am in agreement with much of what Banks is proposing, I see the major contribution that I can make to taking forward some of her arguments as augmenting her views by proposing some alternative perspectives. This will, I hope, serve to deepen the conversation which the lead essay in this edited collection has started. I am particularly interested in Banks' propositions on what may constitute a progressive ethics, and her calls for a reclaiming of the meaning of ethics from the neoliberal position which has appropriated it for its own purposes, and I make some additional suggestions for doing so.

I agree with Banks that ethics in social work has become even more pertinent since the rise of austerity measures and the neoliberal policies, and with Iain Ferguson (2008) that it is worrisome that there is increasing managerialism and marketisation with negative consequences for social work. In an age of audit culture, Banks is quite right when she observes that social workers are increasingly called upon to monitor and evaluate their clients rather than offer them assistance.

Banks alludes to the effects of increasing marketisation, with growing privatisation and the promotion of free markets, resulting in the concentration of power and wealth centrally and in the hands of a few. She also describes how new public management (NPM), characterised by fiscal conservatism, cost efficiency, competitiveness and measurable outputs and throughputs, affected social work in the UK and other Northern countries. She also observes that NPM is changing over time in the light of new public austerity (NPA). I would add that it is not only countries in the North where this has been applied but it has affected those in the South too, such as South Africa. A neoliberal agenda changed the ANC's proposed Reconstruction and Development Programme (RDP), replacing it with more stringent macro-economic policies from the mid-1990s onwards. A global neoliberal trend means that all are subjected to these practices. It is also not just social work that has been affected by this fiscal discipline, but the whole of the human service profession, as well as the higher education sector (see Bozalek and Boughey, 2012) where social workers are educated and trained.

Banks views the growth in the interest in ethics from the 1990s to the 2000s as contradictory, giving rise to two different ways of viewing ethics and NPM – one where the growth of ethics is seen as progressive and critical, reacting against the requirements and consequences of NPM, and the other in which ethics is seen as reinforcing NPM trends. Banks' views of ethics as being both *part of* and *as contestation to* NPM can be likened to Nancy Fraser's (1989) ideas on the politics of needs interpretation. By this Fraser is referring to a discursive contestation about people's needs, which have broken out of the domestic and official/economic spheres into the realm of the *social* where professions like social work exert influence by scrutinising intimate details of people's lives. Fraser argues that the social is a terrain of competing discourses where the market and social movements define needs in different ways. However, Fraser adds a third discourse – that of the expert, which is not included in Banks' two characterisations of ethics, the expert who reinterprets the service user's needs from a therapeutic perspective. Here, the service user perhaps has needs to survive economically and these are reinterpreted by the social worker as psychosocial or interpersonal needs.

Banks notes that the literature on ethical codes and theories that has proliferated since 1990 in social work ethics focuses primarily on principle-based ethics but there is a growing interest in virtue ethics and the ethics of care. In the 1990s and 2000s, national professional associations and regulatory bodies increasingly produced their own extensive codes of social work ethics, in which they make reference to the international definition. Banks claims that these extensive codes are mainly in Northern contexts but South Africa, as an example, as a Southern country also has an extensive (67-page) code of practice (South African Council for Social Service Professions, nd). These codes of ethics have increasingly been used to monitor and evaluate social work, with the rise of NMP and its variants, as well as austerity measures within the failing economies. Efficiency, effectiveness and value for money shown through performance measures and outputs have become the new requirements. In the UK, there has of late been a trend of de-bureaucratising and deregulating social work; however, this has happened together with the austerity measures, leading to a reduction of public services for those in most need. Banks refers to this as the new public austerity (NPA) but for the time being continues to use the term NPM to indicate the influence of increasing marketisation, regulation and measurement of outcomes on social work services. In an interview I conducted with Nancy Fraser in 2011, she points out that, at this particular point in history, the contestation between emancipatory or social movements and social workers is less prevalent in neoliberal times, where the future of the welfare state is uncertain. She also notes that the reprivatisation, pro-market discourse alongside a pro-family discourse has become prevalent in Northern countries such as the United States (Bozalek, 2012).

The ethics which Sarah Banks sees as retrogressive and compliant with NPM is one which reinforces the NPM agenda through four trends which she identifies. The *first trend* is the regulation and disciplining of social workers through professional codes of conduct, which provide elaborate details of what is and what is not permissible

39

behaviour for social workers. The *second trend* is what she terms the 'responsibilisation' of social work, by which she means the ways in which structural issues are depoliticised into personal responsibility. In this way, social workers/their organisations/the state are blamed for negative outcomes and poor quality of services. This is a common strategy in NPM, which holds people responsible for the positions in which they find themselves rather than understanding the larger forces at play (Tronto, 2013). The *third trend* that Banks identifies is similar to the second one, where the individual social worker, the service user or the family are decontextualised and are seen as the focus of attention themselves. Again here ethical dilemmas are framed from a personal rather than political perspective. Fraser refers to this as a 'misframing' of problems, where global issues, for example, are located at a national level, or social policy issues are located at an individual level, thus obscuring the need to take political action regarding a problem (see Bozalek and Boughey, 2012; Fraser, 2012). The *fourth trend* that Banks identifies as being complicit with NPM is where ethics is de-personalised and standardised. Rather than basing relationships on trust, contracts are drawn up between parties, where pre-defined standards and rules are used as a benchmark against which to objectively and impartially measure conformity. This sounds like Rawls' (1971) contract view of social justice. Instead of focusing on the needs of poor and marginalised people, the focus here is achieving effectiveness and efficiency, and the best economic outcomes for a society as a whole.

In the final section of the article, Banks identifies a way of reclaiming and reframing a progressive and radical ethics for social work by locating it in the wider political and social context. She calls this a situated ethics of social justice rather than a political ethics of care, although she sees them as similar. Her reason for this is that she takes social justice as her point of departure and qualifies it with 'situated', rather than care which is qualified with 'political'. She does not really go into the difference between the varieties of social justice and ethics of care approaches, nor does she elaborate on how justice and care may differ or cohere.

She sees ethics as embedded in everyday practices of people's lives rather than abstract principles, which is compatible with Margeret

40

Urban Walker's expressive-collaborative view of ethics, where she 'pictures morality as a socially embodied medium of understanding and adjustment in which people account to each other for the identities, relationships and values that define their responsibilities' (Walker, 1998, p 8). Walker contrasts this interpersonal and collaborative view of ethics with a theoretico-juridical model, which she sees as 'the representation of morality as a compact, propositionally codifiable, impersonally action-guiding code within an agent, or as a compact set of law-like propositions that "explain" the moral behavior of a well-formed moral agent' (Walker, 1998, p 8). Walker identifies theoretico-juridical ethics as informing much of contemporary rights-based ethics.

Banks develops six values for a situated ethics of social justice in social work. These comprise a mixture between moral qualities and action principles which emphasise a relational ontology, solidarity and collective action and enable a resistance and challenge to dominant discourses. These values are: radical social justice; empathetic solidarity; relational autonomy; collective responsibility for resistance; moral courage; and working in and with complexity and contradictions.

With regard to the collective responsibility that Banks refers to, Young's (2011) notion of social connection and responsibility, where we are all implicated in issues of social injustice, is useful. It is forward-looking and non-blaming, but collective responsibility and action is planned. This would mitigate against the responsibilisation of social workers which Banks is concerned about. I would also see Tronto's (1993) notion of privileged irresponsibility and Plumwood's (1993) critique of dualisms as being pertinent for a radical view of ethics. Also, confronting privilege through encounters with difference (Bozalek, 2011) may be useful for a radical social work ethics.

Banks' call for empathic solidarity could benefit from Iris Young's (1997) asymmetrical reciprocity, which assumes that we can never fully understand or put ourselves in the place of another because of our different positioning; we can only be willing to be open to another's embodied subjectivity. Banks' reference to a critical but hopeful position that social workers need to take is valuable, as without critical hope it is difficult to move forward and act (see Bozalek et al, in press, for a more expanded discussion on critical hope and how it differs from hope).

Banks' inclusion of moral courage is important as a value for social work for situations which are uncomfortable, difficult or fear-inducing. Boler and Zembylas's (2003) 'pedagogy of discomfort', which holds that none of us are exempt from hegemonic ideas emanating from dominant discourses and that we need to be discomforted in order to confront these or Davidson's (2004) notion of 'decentering the academic self' in which change is made when encountering difference would be important here.

The final value of Banks' situated ethics of social justice in social work is working in and with complexity and contradictions – here, Val Plumwood's (1993) overcoming dualisms may be pertinent. Banks suggests that social workers need to acknowledge and work with ambivalence, complexity and contradictions rather than seeing things in terms of dichotomous choices in dilemmas. Social workers have to work hard to discover what they need to do and how to question dominant discourses of managerialism and neoliberalism. I particularly like how Banks phrases it as working in the interstices between the contradictions of care and control, 'questioning and challenging, feeling and acting'.

Above all, I see the need to discomfort social workers and encourage them to interrogate their assumptions using normative frameworks such as the ethics of care. It will only be through reflexive practice and by interrogating processes from an ethics of care and social justice perspective such as that of Nancy Fraser and her three-dimensional perspective on justice – looking at affirmative and transformatory practice in relation to recognition, redistribution and representation – that any hope can exist for social work. Furthermore, using Tronto's (2013) five moral elements of care (attentiveness, responsibility, competence, responsiveness and trust) to evaluate practice, alongside her notion of democratic care – in which she asks questions about which social groups are assigned responsibilities and which groups manage to escape these responsibilities, while simultaneously using the services of these caregivers – would be important for ethical considerations in social work. Tronto (2013) calls for the participation of people in assigning caring responsibilities as part of democratic practice.

'Managerialism': challenging the new orthodoxy

Chris Beckett

Sarah Banks' great contribution to social work ethics has been to challenge, as she does here, the idea that 'ethics' is all about solving 'dilemmas' like crossword puzzles, and to offer a much more challenging and dynamic vision of ethical practice as being about courage and a particular kind of hard work. The more I think about this, the more I agree with her. When I look back over my own many shortcomings as a social work practitioner and manager, I can see that very often the things I got wrong were not really about knowing the right thing to do, so much as about having the courage of my convictions, the courage to resist pressure.

All that said, there are many aspects of the lead article here that I find myself wanting to argue with. In particular I feel it subscribes to a kind of myth about the history of social work which I think is very questionable, but which is so commonly found in social work texts that it has become a kind of unexamined orthodoxy. This myth is summed up in Banks' first paragraph, when she speaks of:

> ... the context of increasing managerialism and marketisation in the field of social work in the late 20th and early 21st century – a period that has witnessed an erosion of practice premised on values of social justice and human dignity ... [in which] social workers are increasingly finding themselves expected to monitor and control the behaviour of the growing number of people who are poor, sick and stigmatised.

I started working as a social worker in the early 1980s, before the advent of 'managerialism' and 'marketisation', and I had access to files dating back to the 1970s, 1960s and even earlier. It is not my recollection that this period before managerialism was the Garden of Eden that these accounts imply. Practice then was, it seems to me now, often amateurish and dangerously unaccountable, and frequently oppressive as a result. I think of a case from the 1960s that I encountered in a file, where a woman social worker, responding to allegations that a father was sexually abusing his daughter, had visited the mother and told her she must have sex more often with her husband, so that he wouldn't need to resort to his children. I think of a now infamous residential manager who ran a children's home to which I admitted several children and who has since served a lengthy prison term for abusing children in his care. I think of children spending years in foster homes with no long-term plan at all. I think of inexperienced social workers trying out, without proper training or supervision, fashionable new kinds of therapy on clients who could not say no. I think of rambling and opinionated recording in which service users were described as 'inadequate' and jokes were made at their expense, such as the initials NFN (which stood for 'Normal for Norfolk', and which, when you think about it, is not so very different, ethically, from racism). I think of case conferences that service users were not allowed to attend

Where is the social justice and dignity in all of this? Managerialism is easy to lampoon, and I don't deny that it often distorts practice in grotesque ways, but in some respects what we call managerialism was an attempt to address a real problem. Was it wrong to try to make the best use of limited resources (which is what is meant by the word 'effiency')? Was it wrong to try and make practice more accountable, or to try and measure whether we were making things better or worse? (Bob Pease observes that 'if there is no objective reality, how can we develop the foundations for emancipatory projects?' [2009, p 195]. How can we claim to be on the side of the oppressed, he might have added, if we don't have any means of knowing if we are reducing or increasing their oppression?) Yes, we need to do something about the target culture, the tick boxes, the obsession with assessment at the expense of doing

---

anything that people might actually find helpful. Yes, if social workers are going to achieve anything at all, they need to feel supported in making their own judgements. But let's stop referring back to this mythical golden age in the past, and recognise that what we need to build is something that is new, something that has never yet existed.

Another thing I question in this kind of account is the equation of managerialism with capitalism and free markets. (For one thing, free markets and capitalism are not the same thing, as David Graeber, 2011, points out.) Sarah Banks describes 'economy, efficiency and a concern with maintaining social order' as 'market values', but are they? Wouldn't *any* sensible and ethical system be interested in economy and efficiency (so as to be able to help as many people as possible), and wasn't 'a concern for maintaining social order' famously the obsessive preoccupation of the Soviet Union, the 20th century's first great experiment in running an economy that did *not* work on market principles. (See Spufford, 2011, for a recent imaginative evocation of the strange workings of such an economy.) Managerialism, at its worst, attempts to break down human endeavour into small steps that can be performed by unskilled labour in a routinised way, but this kind of machine-like structure is characteristic both of large capitalist corporations – McDonald's is often cited – and of socialist command economies, and is actually much *less* characteristic of situations which correspond more closely with the theoretical model of a truly 'free market'. (Think of an old-fashioned Arab *souk*, where prices are negotiated between buyers and sellers at every stall: no tick boxes in sight and a lot of very human interactions.)

This may seem a pedantic point to make, but it seems to me that if we are to make progress (and we do need to make progress, for social work has got itself into a very difficult corner), we should stop constructing a composite straw man to attack ('managerialism'), made up of all the different things we dislike or disapprove of, and recognise that there are actually a lot of different and contradictory things going on. Banks quotes a series of key characteristics of new public management (NPM), including 'attention to outputs and performance rather than inputs', 'separation of purchaser and provider', 'breaking down large-scale organisations and using competition to enable "exit" or "choice" by service users', 'decentralisation of budgetary and personal authority to line managers'. She then goes on to suggest that these changes are 'exemplified' by a quote from a social worker talking about 'overbearing procedures ... used as a stick to beat up social workers if a particular procedure hasn't been followed to the letter'. I certainly recognise the problem that the social worker is talking about, and remember, from my own days as a practitioner and front-line manager, the paralysing effects of a culture that is all about following procedures to the letter. That it's a problem, I don't dispute. But I do question whether it exemplifies the characteristics of NPM previously listed. (What has it to do with devolved budgets, for instance? In fact, might not devolved control actually tend to *reduce* this problem of heavy-handed procedures?)

I agree that we need new ways of thinking about social work ethics, ways which deal with both the personal and the political (which, to be honest, cannot be separated), but I'd welcome a more nuanced debate. I don't think it is a question of throwing away *everything* about managerialism, for economy, efficiency, accountability and attention to end results are all desirable things. Nor do I think it is a question of demonising the idea of a mixed economy of care, for small organisations often do have advantages over big ones, and big ones can be dehumanising and bureaucratic, whether they are multi-national corporations or state bureaucracies. As Sarah Banks has touched on, Marx saw morality as essentially an outgrowth of social structure. You get one set of values and ethical priorities in a feudal system, another in a society of hunter-gatherers, another again in a modern capitalist economy. As we grope for better ways of talking and thinking about ethics, we need also to be looking for a new kind of society in which new priorities can emerge. We social work academics, many of us still children of the mid-20th century, can easily become nostalgic about the times in our youth when political battle lines seemed clearer than they do now, and there was a distinction between Right and Left that we all understood, or thought we did. But as we move further into the 21st century, we may need to leave those old battles behind us, as we look for new social structures, outside of the parameters and battle lines of the past.

Ethical practice in an unethical environment

Michael Reisch

Introduction

The ascendant neoliberal paradigm that Banks describes has produced similar effects in the US. The unprecedented centralisation of wealth and power has institutionalised market values throughout society; these include an increased emphasis on outcome measures in the fields of child welfare, criminal justice, public assistance and behavioural health (Soss et al, 2011). Such measures are now a funding requirement of government agencies and major foundations.

The influence of neoliberal values and goals has compelled social workers to reconceptualise their relationship to the state, the market, service users and the community (Reisch, 2009). The shift in focus from personal maintenance to behaviour modification; from long-term stability to short-term outcomes; and from voluntary to compulsory participation has transformed the basic tenets of social work practice and ethics.

Since the 1980s these trends have intensified, particularly after the enactment of 'welfare reform' in 1996. Although its proponents emphasise effectiveness and efficiency, the application of these concepts belies their true intentions. 'Effective' programme outcomes are measured against goals that are predetermined by elites in isolation from their contexts and other services. As Banks asserts, this focus precludes an examination of the larger structural picture.

Similarly, the determination of programmatic 'efficiency' relies exclusively on the application of short-term cost–benefit analysis

---

to the delivery of service 'commodities', although social services are commodities of a distinctly different nature. This narrow, managerial focus ignores the social costs of policy decisions, particularly cutbacks, and the impact of recent economic, demographic and cultural changes on clients' characteristics, needs and patterns of help-seeking and help-utilisation.

Market-oriented values are also reflected in the increased use of resource acquisition as an indicator of personal or organisational success. Funders require programmes serving even marginalised populations to become self-supporting; social work faculties are evaluated by the level of external funding they receive to support their research. The implications of this inversion of means and ends are rarely examined: resource acquisition becomes a primary organisational objective rather than a tool to achieve service goals; the receipt of external grants takes primacy in the determination of scholarly quality over the questions being studied and the *societal* impact of research.

Implications for social work values

In the US, neoliberalism has exalted long-standing individualistic values and denigrated others (community), and promoted scientific, empiricist 'objectivity' (Kirk and Reid, 2002), an ahistorical orientation and the separation of different spheres of society and its institutions. Consequences include increasingly fragmented services, narrower disciplinary specialisations, and greater interorganisational and interprofessional competition within and across sectors (Gronbjerg and Salamon, 2002).

Concurrently, targeting programmes primarily to 'at risk' populations has strengthened popular misconceptions of social services as vehicles for redistributing resources from 'producers' to undeserving recipients. Although polls generally show that social workers are still held in relatively high esteem, recent attacks on government workers (under the guise of fiscal responsibility) and welfare programmes (as dependency-producing 'handouts') undermine this esteem by associating social workers with profligate spending and non-working beneficiaries.

Although these trends create particular challenges for social workers, they have tacitly accepted dominant cultural assumptions without critically examining their ethical implications.

Similarly, the growing corporatisation of universities has transformed students from learners into consumers and revised standards for assessing faculty. In social work, this is reflected in the growing, largely uncritical embrace of evidence-based practice (Thyer, 2007) and the application of outcome measures which reflect a narrow view of professional education (CSWE, 2009).

Ethical discourse

The National Association of Social Workers (NASW, 2008) and International Federation of Social Workers (IFSW, 2010) proclaim that the profession's ethical imperatives include: to provide service; promote social justice; support the dignity and worth of persons; value the importance of human relationships; and act with professional integrity and competence. These underlying principles are admirable, although their call to distribute resources equitably, challenge unjust policies and practices and work in solidarity with marginalised populations is honoured more in the breach than in the observance.

Ironically, most ethical discourse within US social work establishes clear proscriptions regarding professional relationships but only vague prescriptions about promoting social justice. There are several possible explanations for this contradiction. Social workers fear losing their precarious status in the occupational hierarchy if they advocate specific measures to combat injustice (Reisch and Andrews, 2001). There are also conflicting interpretations of social justice even among social workers (Reisch, 2008).

Further, inherent contradictions exist within the profession's dominant values; for example, self-determination is usually expressed in individual, not communal terms. This makes it difficult to reconcile a professional ethos that primarily focuses on clinical practice with individuals with the collective behaviour required to achieve social justice. Potential conflicts between self-determination and other egalitarian goals are also rarely acknowledged. The application of a strengths-based approach inadvertently romanticises people's ability to overcome serious problems without significant external assistance. Under the rubric of 'empowering communities' this argument has rationalised funding cuts for social services.

Conflicts also emerge between egalitarian professional goals and the hierarchical relationships that professional autonomy creates, and between social work's emphasis on 'scientific objectivity' and its subjective values. Finally, there are ongoing conflicts between practitioners' personal and professional values. Although Banks raises valid concerns about this issue, increasingly students' values are more conservative than the profession's stated policy positions (Kelly and Clark, 2009), particularly regarding gay marriage, abortion, affirmative action and redistributive policies.

The master narrative

The co-option of social work ethics by the neoliberal project is reflected in the corruption of the profession's vocabulary; this reinforces dominant societal structures rather than challenging or subverting them. Concepts like empowerment are applied very differently today from their original meaning (Gutierrez et al, 1998). Cultural competence has been established as a practice goal with little examination of what competence means, how competence can become a tool of social control and what the concept competence omits (Ortiz and Jani, 2010). Even advocacy can be used to maintain professional dominance and channel social change within pre-established boundaries if it excludes meaningful opportunities for community participation (Reisch, 2009).

The presence of an unexamined master narrative within the profession abets these processes. Official documents promote the expansion of people's capacity 'to address their own needs', and 'enhance [their] well-being', but emphasise that such changes are more likely to occur 'if *individuals* could be helped to move up and eventually out of the engulfing vortex of personal maladies ... *through improvement of their own moral and physical capacities, with the aid of helpers*' who are 'change agents in society and in the lives of the individuals, families and communities they serve' (IFSW, 2010, emphasis added).

Even the person-in-environment framework subtly reflects this master narrative by implying the separation of the individual from the environment and a sequential, rather than concurrent, impact of environmental forces on human needs (Jani and Reisch, 2011). Social work theories also frequently overlook the influence of history on people's lives. Emphasising research on the effectiveness of established interventions rather than analysing the structural roots of contemporary problems assumes these problems are conditions to be managed rather than eliminated (Webb, 2001).

If social justice is to become more than a rhetorical construct, it is critical to understand the master narrative's implications and how societal institutions construct and reproduce conceptions of 'truth' (Elkins, 2005). Radical social workers can subvert the subtle rationalisation of existing inequalities by helping the profession overcome its fear of resisting those institutions which provide it with sanction and support. In increasingly diverse societies, this challenge is complicated by post-modern critiques (Parton, 2002), growing resistance to the imposition of Western human rights standards (Hunt, 2007; Ife, 2008), and ongoing tensions between respecting the validity of these critiques and the potentially slippery slope of cultural relativism (Akimoto, 2007; Kim, 2007).

Conclusion

An overarching question today for a profession committed to social justice is whether ethical practice is possible in an unethical environment. By presenting a counter-narrative radical social workers can play a crucial role in resolving this dilemma and validating an alternative reality. They can disrupt accepted 'stories' and redefine basic concepts like social justice, cultural competence and empowerment. A key challenge for radical social workers today, therefore, is not merely to create a new narrative but to forge a new social discourse and context within which our stories make sense (Andrews, 2002). By challenging prevailing assumptions about human need and the inevitability of a market-oriented society we can create the space needed to develop alternative frameworks and practice theories (Sandlin and Clark, 2009). By posing different research questions, we can clarify ambiguities in social work's fundamental concepts and vocabulary. By suggesting new practice roles, we can form new alliances with clients and potential allies in the pursuit of social justice. This would require, however, a revolution in values and ethics both inside and outside the academy.

Social work ethics and social justice: the growing gap

Fumihito Ito

Introduction

No one can deny the statement that social work is an ethical career (Ferguson, 2008). As the international definition of social work declared in 2000, social work is concerned with promoting human rights and social justice, something that is also accepted within the Japanese profession. Nakamura's book, for example, refers to 'the ethics of social work: principles and standards' and includes a translation of materials adopted by the International Federation of Social Work (IFSW) since 1994 (Nakamura and Japanese Association of Social Workers, 1999). It is clear that social work cannot exist without an ethical awareness.

It is curious and surprising, therefore, that nowhere did the term 'social justice' appear in the Japanese code of ethics, adopted by the four main associations of professional social workers in Japan, which was published as late as 1995 (Nakamura and Japanese Association of Social Workers, 1999). It is of course possible to read the meaning of 'social justice' into the code if you scrutinise it carefully enough but why was this crucial term not written explicitly into this code of ethics? In fact, it was as recently as eight years ago (2005) that the term 'social justice' was added in accordance with the international definition of social work approved by the IFSW in 2000. By contrast, Ferguson (2008) argues that social work's concern with promoting social justice has been present since its beginnings and has been enriched and encouraged through its contact with social movements.

One explanation is that, under attack from the ideology of New Public Management (NPM) or 'managerialism', it is no exaggeration to say that Japanese social work has been on the political defensive during the last 15 years. In spite of the fact that some social workers have personally engaged with clients in social action, it is concerning that all the professional associations of social work have been relatively silent regarding the political aspect of social work as a social movement or what the role of social work should be (Yokoyama et al, 2011).

This situation leads us to the next question: how many Japanese academics and practitioners really recognise *the interdependent relationship* between the notion of 'social justice' on the one hand and the notion of 'ethics' as the core value of social work on the other? This article will explore how the ethics of social work have been or should be dealt with in the context of neoliberal managerial policies by focusing on the 'divergence' of social work ethics between the political/practice level and the theoretical level in the context of Japan.

'Ethics of social justice' and 'ethics of care'

Banks explains in her lead article how we understand the term 'ethics' in the broader sense. This can be classified into four dimensions: (1) conduct; (2) character; (3) relationship and (4) the good society. In this classification, 'ethics of social justice' applies to (1) and (4), whilst 'ethics of care' relates to (2) and (3). According to this, it is clear that an act of promoting social justice becomes an ethical matter. In fact, Banks argues that social justice corresponds to 'an ethical practice that is driven by a response to situated injustice and wrongs' from Critchley (2007). Not surprisingly, in this definition radical social work is an ethical activity.

NPM and the dialectic of care and control

Banks' analysis shows that the emergence of 'the ethics boom' in social work literature stems from a process of polarisation in social work, with NPM as its intermediary. She observes that many ethical principles and standards in social work (especially) in the English-speaking world have become longer and more detailed and suggests that in some respects this trend can be seen as a positive reform, contributing to the protection of human rights for clients . At the same time, however, she also evaluates this revision sceptically as involving the erosion of professional discretion and the creation of narrow-minded practice based on self-censorship.

It is necessary to understand social work within the context of 'the dialectic of care and control'. Banks describes the importance of reclaiming ethics of social work in age of austerity:

> [The] account of social work as part of the state-organised welfare provision is important as it helps us understand how some of the ethical issues are inherent in the role of the social worker. … it is based on contradictions and social ambivalence. Social work contributes towards expressing society's altruism (care) and enforcing societal norms (control); it champions individual rights as well as protecting the collective good. … As the welfare state is questioned, undermined and reformed, so the role of social work is also subject to question and change. (Banks, 2006, p 20)

This interpretation is supported not only by Banks but also by other critical academics (Thompson, 2000; Ferguson and Lavalette, 2009). Social work as an agent of the welfare state should be better understood within this context. It suggests that social work practice inevitably faces ethical dilemmas stemming from its ambivalent role.

NPM has reinforced a social work practice aimed at increasing social control. The basic trend of reform of social services over the last two decades can be analysed as: (1) the marketisation of social services within a business ethos (cost-effectiveness, efficiency and competition); (2) greater emphasis on 'accountability' based on the introduction of 'evidence-based practice' (EBP) and its attainments, with bureaucratic fragmentation of implementing procedures (measurement, outcomes and achievement); and (3) a 'deskilling' of the profession (the loss of its own discretion and autonomy for good practice) as the result, according to Banks (see also Dustin, 2007).

Furthermore, Banks compares and contrasts testimony from several practitioners, as well as from Professor Eileen Munro. Munro has posed a crucial question as to how social service provision can address human needs in a context obsessed with budget control management and suggests that the domination of this approach, far from reducing need, has contributed to increased 'standardisation' of social services.

Certainly the hope of state managers would be that social workers as statutory agents should carry out their work in accordance with the state's wishes since the state needs to demonstrate to the taxpayer a 'responsible' attitude towards the provision of services. However, the social worker is not a mere service provider and gatekeeper. Thus, examining the core values of social work, it is necessary to revise and rethink how we deal with ethics in broader sense.

Banks is very aware of the need to rethink social work ethics due to the polarisation that NPM has created. This division can be characterised as 'progressive and critical of NPM' and as 'regressive and compliant with NPM' respectively. However, both phenomena should not always be seen as mutually exclusive but rather as the mirror image of the 'dialectic of care and social control'. Thus, the truth of social workers' dilemmas on the front line lies at the borderline of both spheres. Put differently, social work practice can either resist the neoliberal policies underpinned by managerialism or be subordinate to the authority of NPM. As Banks points out, whether or not social workers become ethical carriers or gatekeepers, it 'is up to us to ensure that these [radical rhetoric] values can be translated into practice and show how this can be done, and is being done, by many social workers around the world'.

Ethics of social work in Japanese context: a deviance of theoretical and political?

In Japan, managerial policies based on a care management approach have overwhelmingly covered all fields of social services since 2000. Older people have been the most important subjects of this policy. The introduction of the 'public care insurance scheme' in 2000 was very adaptable to care management. Its methodology has been accepted and welcomed by the state in that it was easily adaptable to budget control (Kosaka, 2011). In stark contrast to the increased discussion of ethics at a theoretical level, many care managers have willingly committed to following regulations and guidelines encouraged by state.

Here is a typical example from Japan of the subordination of the social work profession to the authority of NPM. A paper entitled 'Care management practice: how do we make an appropriate care plan from the view point of the care manager?', sent to participants in a workshop, allows us to understand the true extent to which care management is the product of NPM ideology. Although the public ideal of care management was to promote real independence for clients, the author of this paper explains that care management is essential for the purposes of fraud reduction and budgetary control:

> Central government introduced the cuts policy since 2004 and this policy has encouraged maintaining the [care management] scheme in action ... The ministry encouraged a reduction target for all local authorities by 2008 ... because of inadequate budget and ageing, it is very important to administer the scheme ... service users need to become good consumers. (Nakazawa, 2012, pp 1, 4, 5)

Apparently Nakazawa argues that care management makes a contribution to fiscal discipline by teaching the service user the limitation of the budget. Surprisingly, he also stresses that this kind of care management actually contributes to the ethics of social work and in fact writes not only as a qualified social worker but also as the chairman of ethics of the social work committee of the association of care managers! Presumably there have been many such workshops all over Japan, aimed at turning qualified good practitioners into care managers.

Examples such as this suggest that in Japan notions of social justice and ethical practice are seen as completely separate elements. It is perhaps more accurate to suggest, however, that while Japanese social work has a heavy *theoretical* emphasis on important ethical aspects of social work, this is sometimes accompanied by a dismissive *political* attitude to wider issues of social justice.

Concluding comments

The divergence referred to above suggests that for the Japanese social work profession, accepting the notion of social justice has historically involved some difficulty and hesitation (Ito, 2011). It also implies that there has been a growing gap between theoretical understandings of ethics on the one hand and the political and professional praxis of social work on the other, in that many front-line practitioners have seen addressing the needs of the individual client and providing services as their sole ethical duty. Of course, many social workers, perhaps even 'the silent majority', would quite possibly accept Banks' radical suggestions and proposals for ethics in social work theoretically and practically. At present, however, it is very difficult to reach agreement as a profession on a clear 'mission statement' concerning the political role of the social worker and to whom he or she is accountable. That said, this will not stop some of us from seeking to reclaim a social work ethics which can effectively challenge the priorities of NPM.

Working in the spaces between care and control

Merlinda Weinberg

Introduction

Dr Banks has written a compelling and cogent piece on the need to reclaim a progressive vision of ethics for social work. Particularly significant are her calls to broaden the definition of ethics by recognising relationships as the bedrock for ethical behaviour and politicising our understanding of ethics. She does an excellent job of linking the New Public Management (NPM) with contradictory trends in ethics that can have either liberatory or reactionary potentials. Her exhortation of the types of actions and qualities that can reclaim ethics as situated and political is a road map for an agenda aiming towards social justice.

The inadequacies of a principle-based codes approach to ethics

There are several amplifications and additions that I would like to provide. The first relates to Dr Banks' point that one direction ethics has taken in social work has been a 'conformity to prevailing social norms and regulations', usually bolstered by a reliance on principle-based codes of ethics. This canonical view of ethics focuses on the responsibility of the autonomous individual, in an impersonal and context-free way, assuming that a set of guidelines can be universally provided that will lead to right action. It has been suggested that the traditional orientation is problematic because it privileges sameness and repeatability (Walker, 1998, p 53) and eviscerates the very historical context, collaboration and relationality necessary to ethical functioning that Banks promotes. And, 'code-oriented moralities tend to normalize principle because rather than continually questioning proper conduct they express a desire to find the true ground of our being' (Orlie, 1997, p 195). I think what is meant by the 'true ground of our being' is the essence of who we ought to be as moral actors. Since that is not possible, a code of ethics based on a fixed list of principles can lead to dogma, coercion and the abdication of personal morality and responsibility (Asquith and Rice, 2005).

Ethical trespass

Furthermore, there are theorists who claim that no matter how good our intentions and actions, there will be ethical trespass. This term was coined by Hannah Arendt (1958) and has been expanded by Melissa Orlie (1997). These theorists are referring to the harm humans perpetrate, not from malevolent aims but due to 'our participation in social processes and identities' (Orlie, 1997, p 5). Social processes include determining who is sick and who is well; who is judged to be adequate as a parent and who is not, as examples. And those most likely to harm are those individuals dominant in relations of ruling (Smith, 1990). Social workers, through their responsibilities as agents of the state, through the judgements they execute and the norms they perpetuate, are those players (Weinberg, 2006). Orlie argues that we can never know the total ramifications of any decision we render and that there may be unanticipated harms attached. This is even more the case when there are contradictory elements to those decisions. One such element in social work is the fact that usually there is more than one service user to whom practitioners must respond simultaneously and these individuals may have conflicting needs and desires. Consequently, ethics must always include 'moral courage' and humility, recognising fallibility, and living with the reality of complexity and contradictions, as Banks endorses.

Bringing in the voices of the marginalised

When a vision of ethics is based on norms, those norms will be constructed on the actions of some moral agents. But there will always be subordinated identities that a normative code does not include or, worse, negates (Walker, 1998). Currently I am engaged in a qualitative research study around ethics in social work practice, interviewing front-line practitioners. One of the most significant findings has been that social workers who self-identified as marginalised on some dimension (for example on the basis of racial–ethnic identity or as rural practitioners) often had divergent or adjunctive views from those promulgated in their jurisdictional codes of ethics. As an illustration, one status[1] Aboriginal practitioner discussed the following:

> ... the ethical dilemma isn't in the duty to report. It's what happens after the duty to report. That you set a whole mechanism in place that doesn't recognize ... I can say this especially for First Nation[s] ... the history of why someone would act in the way that they do. That doesn't recognize the disrupted attachment ... the impact of generational trauma... I mean most people would say OK, duty to report, straightforward, we need to do this. I think what happens is what you carry with you after you follow through on a duty to report ... the ... broken relationship, then how do you rebuild the trust ... in a clinical relationship again?

In this quote, the insufficiency of codes for ethical behaviour is revealed. For this worker, the emphasis is on context and the unique history of the service user; also on what happens *after* the utilisation of codes in the relational space between client and worker. Principles are only useful to the degree to which they are acted upon to support justice and social inclusion. While one could argue that a white worker might well have expressed similar views, and essentialised notions of identity are problematic, I believe that those who claim to be on the margins, at moments, bring a standpoint (Harding, 2004; Intemann, 2010) that allows them to perceive what is missing or wrong with the dominant perspectives and nourishes resistance (hooks, 1990, quoted in Hekman, 1995). Multiplicity enriches our understanding of ethics. A reclaimed social work ethics must welcome those subjugated voices, both practitioners' and service users', and find ways to incorporate their lessons and perspectives.

The bifurcation of ethics and politics

A significant point raised by Dr Banks is that themes of human needs, relationships, equality and justice 'are not labelled as "ethical' themes" but as "political"'). While this quote was referring specifically to the writings of Marx, I believe the same bifurcation of what is political and what is ethical exists in our current neoliberal context. And social workers maintain that split for a variety of reasons: due to the conceptual divisions between clinical, community and policy streams; from the emphasis in practice on the dyad of worker/client separated from the broader social environment; to preserve 'innocence' from the need to act on social transformation and to maintain the benefits that accrue from privilege as professionals (Weinberg, 2010). By keeping the notion of ethics as separate from the political context in which social workers operate, the status quo is maintained and a society of haves and have-nots is perpetuated, an argument that Banks addresses when she states the need to question the 'power and interests of governments, public service employers, private corporations and social workers themselves that cause them to ignore or accept inequalities and oppression'. I believe that no ethics is value-free and that there is eternally a political element to ethical deliberations, since there are always power dimensions and material benefits at stake. Consequently, eliminating the divide between ethics and politics is essential, a 'politicised ethics', as Banks advocates.

New Public Management and gender: exploitation and the disavowal of emotion

That politicised view begins by understanding the context in which practice occurs. The features of the NPM have been well laid out by Dr Banks, including more time spent on efficiencies, accountability and the avoidance of risk (Meagher and Parton, 2004; Burton and van den Broek, 2009; Healy, 2009) while less time is available for autonomous, creative practice focused on clients. In addition to the four regressive effects on ethics that Banks lists, I would like to add a fifth. In order to accomplish the work that practitioners view as sound and ethical, they often put in time beyond their actual work hours to ensure that service users receive the perceived needed service. As an illustration from the same study mentioned above, the following exchange occurred:

> INTERVIEWER: ... you were talking about, one of the ethical dilemmas for you was the paperwork and that it required you to be putting in way more time around the paperwork than actually seeing clients.... And I wondered how you dealt with that?
>
> PARTICIPANT: Weekends. ... I would work 13 hours a day ...
>
> INTERVIEWER: Wow!
>
> ...
>
> PARTICIPANT: So, yeah ... I'd stay at the clinic till nine o'clock at night, I'd come in on the weekends to get it done ...
>
> INTERVIEWER: Jeeze.
>
> PARTICIPANT: And I'm not alone in that.

The dynamic of going above and beyond to ensure ethical practice results in an exploitation of the workers (Healy, 2009; Baines et al, 2011)

---

on whose backs the NPM survives and thrives. This is a gendered effect, in part due to emphasis on the values of caring and the ambivalence that the social work profession has towards professionalisation (Healy, 2009). Although the profession is dominated by women, these attitudes are not essential features of women or men. Meagher and Parton (2004) contend that managerialism is a masculinist project. By this they mean that the principles and ideals traditionally associated with being masculine, such as valuing justice over care, objectivity over subjective evaluations, reason over emotion, are privileged, and it is in this sense that I am referring to the gendered effects.

An additional gendered aspect of the NPM is the disavowal of emotion as an important component in ethical practice. Moral philosophers and psychologists have long debated the role of feelings in ethical decision-making; with some seeing emotion as an impediment, and others as significant in the formation of virtue and correct ethical judgements (Kristjánsson, 2009; Coplan, 2010; Craigie, 2011). Although there are risks to relying on non-rational processes (Rogerson et al, 2011), emotions can signal the moral distress a practitioner feels on those occasions when what s/he wants to do seems blocked by institutional constraints (Weinberg, 2009). Moreover, Vetlesen has suggested that '*the emotional bond is not morally neutral*' (1994, p 179, emphasis in original). It is this emotional bond that potentially may be violated or suspended when one adopts an attitude of objectivity in practice. Consequently, I support Dr Banks' stance that emotion must be encompassed in ethics.

Conclusion

The profession of social work is rife with endemic paradoxes such as the societal responsibility for both care and the discipline of others . And the growth of interest in ethics can either be a salutary or destructive effect of the NPM, as Banks contends. While these paradoxes are part of the complexities of the profession and of responding ethically, they are also part of the promise. For where there is ambiguity, there is also room to manoeuvre and resist. In crisis theory there is a tenet that there is more possibility for change during crisis than when people are satisfied. NPM presents such a crisis in social work. Banks suggests that social workers need to work 'in the spaces between the contradictions of care and control', one of those intrinsic social work paradoxes, and through her articulation of the issues she has opened up some admirable spaces for reclaiming ethics for a progressive social work.

Note

[1] The term applies to federally registered Canadian Aboriginal people who have special status and certain privileges under the laws of Canada.

A Marxist perspective

Paul Blackledge

Sarah Banks' opening contribution to this collection is appealing in part because of her expansive category of ethics. Indeed, by contrast with the dominant tendency within academia she even acknowledges that Marx's views on the subject deserve a hearing. If there is a weakness with her article it is perhaps that she doesn't develop this insight far enough. In particular I think that had she thought more about Marx's concept of alienation she might be more critical of the idea that resistance to austerity can be based upon the core values of social work. As we shall see, it is not that this idea is without legs; it is rather that it needs to be handled carefully.

Marx's ethics is often misconstrued because it involves a profound challenge to the clear delineation between science and ethics that is taken as axiomatic within post-Kantian moral theory. *Capital* (Marx, 1975) is simultaneously scientific, ethical and political in scope, and this reflects Marx's view that because we interpret the world from concrete, socially determined standpoints it is impossible to unpick what we know of it from our ethically saturated forms of practice within it. From this perspective, modern moral theory's attempt to separate factual and value statements is not simply wrong, more profoundly it represents a naturalisation of the socially determined standpoint of the individual within civil society. The power of the nihilist critique of morality stems from Nietzsche's recognition that we do interpret the world from particular perspectives, but because he too naturalises the standpoint of egoistic individualism his critique of morality is best understood less as a radical alternative to the moral standpoint than as the flipside of the same error: by naturalising egoistic individualism neither approach is able to see beyond an emotivist context within

71

which morality has been reduced to individual opinion. This is why Alasdair MacIntyre bemoans the modern moral condition as a simulacrum of classical ethics.

MacIntyre's alternative practice-based ethics shares some similarities with Banks' comments on the ethics of social work. According to MacIntyre, a practice is any complex form of human activity through which goods internal to that activity are realised as practitioners strive to excel at it. Clearly social work would count as a MacIntyrean practice. However, as will become evident below there are problems with this approach that illuminate weaknesses with Banks' account of social work ethics. MacIntyre developed his ideas through a critique of Marx, and in particular against the backdrop of his disillusion with Marx's conception of the working class. According to Marx, working-class struggles against capitalism provide a concrete standpoint from which to criticise liberalism's naturalisation of egoistic individualism. By contrast with the way modern morality is unable, for instance through Kant's concept of asocial sociality, to conceive the social except negatively as alienation, the standpoint of the working class provides Marx with the resources necessary to grasp both the historically specific nature of modern capitalist social relations and the concrete modern form by which we express our social individuality in rebellion against this condition. And, as against modern (liberal) moral theory's empty conceptions of rights and duties and so on, because Marx's ethics draws on Hegel's synthesis of Aristotle's objective ethics of human flourishing with Kant's conception of human freedom, his model of freedom is rooted in collective working-class struggles for democracy against alienation; it has a concrete social content.

There is, of course, a broad overlap between this model and Banks' focus on the twin issues of austerity and neoliberalism. She would undoubtedly agree that these policies not only worsen the context within which social workers operate, but also serve to deny the social aspect of our nature by reducing us to the status of mere consumers. And Banks is right to point out that much of what counts as ethics in contemporary social work is best understood as a series of rules by which new forms of managerialism are embedded within the welfare state. Where she is weaker is on the alternative ethics she suggests has emerged in opposition to neoliberal managerialism.

There are, I think, two problems with her argument. First, there is no sense in her account of the turn to ethics from the 1970s and 1980s onwards that this process reflected, in part, the Left's retreat from politics in a context of defeats for the workers' movement in this period. As the movements of the 1960s and 1970s ebbed there was an associated tendency for theory to retreat from politics to ethics, and in particular to one or other form of Kantianism. The problem with morality thus conceived was not so much that it tended towards what Marx, following Fourier, called 'impotence in action', but more insidiously that its top-down essence dovetailed with increasingly authoritarian forms of statist politics. For many it was a series of all too short steps from forms of ethical socialism in the 1970s through a kind of moralistic reformism in the 1980s to the new managerialism and associated pseudo-leftist variants on the moral underclass discourse in the 1990s and beyond.

If this process suggests the Left should be wary of ethical politics, the other weakness with Banks' argument reflects a similarly ambiguous relationship to statist politics. To claim that resistance to austerity should start from the core values of social work skirts over the contradictory nature not only of social work but also of the welfare state more generally. Although states are often counterposed to markets, the apparent autonomy of modern states is better understood as part of broader capitalist relations rooted in the wage form. Whereas exploitation in pre-capitalist societies took directly political forms, because the exploitation of wage labour occurs within the production process itself, it does not necessitate direct political supervision.

Although this situation creates the potential for the modern separation between politics (state) and economics (markets), it would be a mistake to suppose that it means states are non-capitalist institutions. Modern states are structurally interdependent with capital and emerge to reproduce the conditions of capital accumulation. Social work is best understood from this perspective as a part of a broader set of structures designed to reproduce capitalist social relations in general

73

and the labour force in particular. So long as there have been social workers there have been debates about how best to do this. But it should not be forgotten that a key driver of debates over the nature of social work going back as far as the Fabian challenge to the Charity Organisation Society in the 19th century was the need to efficiently reproduce labour in the context of international competition.

Of course, because it is characterised by such debates social work creates a space within which much more radical ideas might flourish. However, these have always been a minority within the profession. This was true even in the 1970s when, in the wake of two decades of boom which informed both a doubling in funding for personal social services alongside a degree of political radicalisation among its practitioners, a door was opened to an expansion and deepening of the critical, caring aspect of social work. If the subsequent cuts to social services have inevitably come into conflict with this aspect of the job, it is important to recognise that the cuts were underpinned by the same logic that previously had fostered the emergence of the welfare state: the need to reproduce labour as efficiently as possible in the context of international competition.

The problem with taking social work or even the welfare state more broadly as the basis for a critique of austerity is, contra MacIntyre's conception of practice, that these activities emerged as an alienated expression of the need to help reproduce labour power. Indeed, it is because the state and the market are best understood as two sides of the same process of alienation that neither the welfare state nor one or other of its constituent parts are able to act as a systematic basis for emancipatory critique. This is not to dismiss the contributions that might be made from within social work. Rather it is to recognise that although welfare states represent a partial negation of capitalism's tendency to commodify all aspects of modern life, they do so on the basis of this tendency. So while they create a space of non-commodified relations, they are nevertheless structurally interdependent with capital.

While this argument implies that the 'core values of social work' are more ambiguous than Banks admits, it is undoubtedly right that managerialism and austerity conflict not only with radical aspects of social work practice but also with more mainstream aspects of the profession. If this conflict creates a space for a debate about how best to defend social work, my point is that it would be a mistake to confine this debate to narrow issues of social work itself. The scale of the attacks on the working class as a whole opens the door to renewal of the kinds of political trade unionism which inspired radical social work in the 1970s and through which contemporary social workers might help build real bonds of solidarity across the working class as a whole as a concrete negation of alienation.

Reflections on the responses to 'Reclaiming social work ethics'

Sarah Banks

It is a privilege to have the opportunity to read and reflect on the thoughtful and sometimes challenging responses to the opening essay in this book. In these short concluding comments I will pick up on just a few of the valuable criticisms, comments and questions raised.

International perspectives

One of the interesting features of the responses is that the authors bring perspectives from a range of countries – elaborating on the impact of tendencies towards the new public management (NPM) across different continents. Their accounts suggest that the broad trends are global, although the implications play out differently depending on national and cultural contexts. Ito, for example, offers an analysis of the position of social work in Japan using the introduction of care management as an illustration of the imperative towards cost-cutting and the framing of service users as 'good (budget-conscious) consumers'. Bozalek challenges the suggestion that long codes of ethics and practice are confined to countries in the global North, citing the example of the 67-page code of practice for South African social services professions. Based on her research with Canadian social workers, Weinberg stresses the importance of bringing in the voices of marginalised people, including status Aboriginal social workers, whose perspectives are often unrepresented in the prevailing discourse of social work ethics. Reisch usefully elaborates the ascendency of the neoliberal paradigm in the US, arguing that market values have become institutionalised in all aspects of life and that there is a role for social work in developing a counter-discourse; while Reamer offers an important account of the historical development of thinking and practice around ethics in social work which, while not specifically located, clearly reflects the dominant Anglo-American experience.

Turning to the UK context, Cowden elaborates further the profound implications of NPM for social work ethics, the role of the New Labour government in developing more punitive and controlling conceptions of welfare and the dangers posed by the colonisation of the progressive language of social work by neoliberal discourse. Beckett, by contrast, draws upon his experience of working as a social worker in the UK to assert some of the benefits of managerialism for ethical practice in social work. Finally Blackledge reminds us of debates in early British social work between the Fabians and the Charity Organisation Society in the context of his Marxist analysis of the role of social work in a capitalist state.

Challenges to 'Reclaiming social work ethics'

Many of the responses are in broad agreement with the ideas of the opening article, elaborating on the arguments, pointing to gaps and proposing further arguments that could be developed or perspectives that should be added. All except Blackledge are writing from inside social work. The most direct and challenging critiques come from Blackledge (from outside social work with an explicitly Marxist perspective) and Beckett (from inside social work drawing on his practice experience). The implications of both critiques, albeit in different ways, are to challenge the call to 'reclaim' social work ethics. Beckett sees this call as urging a return to a 'golden age' of social work before the grip of the new managerialism and marketisation took hold. Against this picture of current social work, he argues that managerialism can result in fairer and more respectful practice and doubts that social

—

work in the past was any better (and may have been worse) than at the present time. Blackledge makes the more challenging point that given the rationale for social work (as part of the welfare state) is to reproduce capitalist social relations, then it is not possible to base a critique of austerity on existing social work values.

These two lines of criticism highlight the ambiguity of the call to 'reclaim' social work ethics and the need to rethink and tighten up what is meant by this. 'Reclaiming' can be taken literally to mean taking back something that existed in the past in the form that it existed previously. However, in the context of social movements and marginalised groups, to 'reclaim' a concept, value or space often means not just taking back, but redefining, reinterpreting or inhabiting concepts and spaces in new ways – for example, 'reclaiming the night' (for women to inhabit without fear) or 'reclaiming the term "Black"' (for people of colour to self-describe in a political, non-stigmatising sense). Hence 'reclaiming social work', 'reclaiming social work values' and 'reclaiming social work ethics' should be constructed in the same way – not just as rediscovering and re-appropriating what once was, but also reinterpreting what once was and laying claim to a new perspective, position or space.

However, in the lead article, I do not distinguish these senses of 'reclaiming'. I talk of 'resisting the attacks on the core values of social work' and 'reasserting its value base'. Yet, as many of the other contributors to the book testify, the values of social work are contested, contradictory and changing. So to call for return to the 'core values of social work' is ambiguous (which values?) and potentially dangerous (all social work values are not 'progressive' or 'radical'). It is a seductive call to make, as it potentially reaches and resonates with many social workers – not just those who identify themselves as radical. This is because the impact of NPM and neoliberal ideology has permeated social work to such an extent (as argued by Reisch and Cowden) that a significant majority of social workers are alienated from their work (both in the Marxist sense suggested by Blackledge, as well as simply burnt out). Hence they will rally to the call of 'we didn't come into social work for this' (see Lavalette's [2011, pp 9–10] account of the development of the Social Work Action Network). For social workers are finding it increasingly difficult to practise by the old liberal and social democratic values based on respectful care and fair treatment, let alone a more radical version of social justice.

Yet it is important to make clear that it is the reclaiming of what Ferguson and Woodward (2009, pp 13–32) call the 'radical kernel' in social work (radical social justice) that is being referred to in this context. And the process of 'reclaiming' should not comprise just going back to an earlier version of social justice, but reinterpreting it in a 21st-century context and claiming a new distinct space for radical social work. This new space entails that the old values relating to the valuing of human dignity and possibility of developing respectful relationships of care and trust are not interpreted simply in terms of individual rights to choice over a limited range of residual services, but in conjunction with a radical version of social justice that challenges the framing of welfare benefits as compensation for idle, poor or inadequate people and offers an analysis of structural inequalities.

While Beckett is certainly right that aspects of managerialism (eg eligibility criteria, monitored standards and targets for delivery of services) may result in practice that is fairer, more accountable and respectful to service users, it is specifically the *new* managerialism (often referred to in the context of welfare services as the *new public management*) that is the focus of the lead article. NPM is more than just bureaucracy; it is explicitly framed in terms of market values of competition (whether internal/'quasi' or external markets), consumerism and individual choice. For this reason NPM brings into sharp focus the contradictions on which the welfare state is based – discomforting social workers (see Bozalek's response), as the always fragile balance between welfare and capitalism, solidarity and self-help, collectivism and individualism tips more heavily towards the latter. This is also the reason that Blackledge is right that to couch the call for resistance in terms of returning to the core values of social work will not work if what we are aiming for is a radical social work that challenges the ideology that provides the rationale for social work itself. We require a much more serious 'reclaiming' (that goes beyond 'returning') for a radical social work to be possible.

The possibility of radical social work?

A questioning of whether the concept of radical social work makes sense is a broader implication of Blackledge's critique and is one with which advocates of radical social work have long grappled (from Corrigan and Leonard,1978, to Ferguson, 2008, along with many of the contributors to this volume).

Yet many of the contributors to this book and others within social work do see the possibility of a different kind of social work playing a role in the transformation of social relations. They present arguments for how this might be achieved, including: using the contradictions inherent in welfare-capitalism (Ito; Weinberg); critiquing dominant narratives (Cowden; Reisch; Weinberg); developing counter-narratives or discourses (Reisch); working for prefigurative micro-level changes (Langan and Lee, 1989); and building alliances with service users, other welfare workers, trade unions and social movements (Corrigan and Leonard, 1978; Ferguson, 2008). Indeed, Blackledge acknowledges the potential for social workers to contribute to the renewal of trade unionism and building bonds of solidarity. Whether this can be done from the uncomfortable position of being located both 'in and against the state' (London Edinburgh Weekend Return Group, 1980) is still a subject of debate among social workers on the Left. As the spaces for resistance within social work get smaller, the impetus for resistance is increasing, and new alliances between social workers, trade unions, service users and other social movements are developing – whether this be in the context of rallies against local authority cuts in the UK, street protests in Greece or the Occupy! movement in Ljubljana mentioned in the lead article.

To those on the Left outside social work (and many inside) the radical social work project may seem both idealistic (it can never be achieved) and misguided (it diverts attention from real struggles and, despite the best intentions, reinforces existing capitalist social relations).

—

Hence it is important to continue to acknowledge the position of social work at the heart of the contradictions of welfare-capitalism and that its potential for reinforcing the status quo is much greater than its potential for radical change. Nevertheless, for those of us who are not revolutionary Marxists, but who are committed to radical evolutionary change based on social justice, social work is one site where that struggle can be joined – both as social workers and as, and alongside, activists in the green, feminist, disability, anti-racist, anti-capitalist and other social movements.

What next for social work ethics?

Reamer, in his useful historical account of the changing approaches to social work ethics, raises the question as to whether we are now about to enter, or whether I would advocate that we should enter, a 'post-modern' period. In the field of moral philosophy, 'post-modernism' is sometimes associated with 'the end of ethics'. However, it is perhaps best understood as meaning the end of a particular version of ethics – based on universal and foundational theories applicable in all times, places and circumstances (such as Kantianism or utilitarianism). One version of 'post-modern ethics' would be a situated ethics, rooted in particular times, places and situations, and hence deeply contextualised. 'Situated ethics' is certainly a feature of the lead article and so I can see why Reamer makes this suggestion about post-modernism. Yet, as Reisch comments, we also need to avoid the dangers of (ethical) relativism, which often accompanies post-modernist accounts.

It would require another chapter to explore the potential and pitfalls of versions of critical post-modernism (briefly touched on in Banks, 2012, pp 84–7; see also Ferguson, 2008, pp 107–18; Leonard, 1995, 1997) and to defend the outline at the end of the lead article of a 'situated ethics of social justice'. Bozalek is right in commenting (that there is a need for more discussion of the relationship between the ethics of care and the ethics of justice. There is also a need for more work to develop the 'situated ethics of social justice' proposed in the lead article and its relationship to the 'political ethics of care' developed by Tronto (1993) and others. At this point I can only repeat the importance of starting with social justice (as opposed to the relationship of care between two people) as a way of ensuring that collectivity and solidarity are at the heart of ethics, rather than 'bolted on' or seen as a political context for care. Both a political ethics of care and a situated ethics of social justice are premised on the importance of the personal and impersonal, situated and principled, rational and emotional dimensions of ethics. As argued elsewhere, these are complementary and may often be in a dialectical relationship with each other (Banks, 2004, pp 98–105, 149–78; Banks, 2007; 2013).

The provocative, constructive and critical elaborations offered by the respondents to the lead article are an invaluable contribution to ongoing debates about social work ethics, the possibility of radical social work and its role in broader society in a time of austerity. I would like to conclude by drawing attention to the role of the Social Work Action Network (http://socialworkfuture.org), the popularity of which stems from its broad call to reclaim both the traditional caring values of social work as well as a commitment to progressive social justice. Like many social movements, it draws people from a range of political backgrounds and allegiances and is an important arena in which the values and ethics for a progressive social work can be debated and developed.

References

Akimoto, T. (2007) 'Social justice and social welfare policies beyond national boundaries: What should we question?', in *Human rights and social justice: Rethinking social welfare's mission*, Seoul: Korean Academy of Social Welfare, pp 59–74.

Andrews, M. (2002) 'Introduction: Counter-narratives and the power to oppose', *Narrative Inquiry*, vol 12, no 1, pp 1–6.

Arendt, H. (1958) *The human condition*, Chicago: University of Chicago Press.

Asquith, M. and Rice, K. (2005) 'Social work ethics – practice and practitioners', *New Global Development: JI & CSW*, vol 21, no 1, pp 10–17.

Australian Association of Social Workers (1989) *Code of ethics: By-laws on ethics*, Hawker: Australian Association of Social Workers.

Australian Association of Social Workers (2010) *Code of ethics*, Canberra: Australian Association of Social Workers.

Bailey, R. and Brake, M. (eds) (1975) *Radical social work*, London: Edward Arnold.

Baines, D., Cunningham, I. and Fraser, H. (2011) 'Constrained by managerialism: caring as participation in the voluntary social services', *Economic and Industrial Democracy*, vol 32, no 2, pp 329–52.

Baistow, K. (1994) 'Liberation and regulation? Some paradoxes of empowerment', *Critical Social Policy* vol 14, no 42, pp 34-46.

Banks, S. (2004) *Ethics, accountability and the social professions*, Basingstoke: Palgrave Macmillan.

Banks, S. (2006) *Ethics and values in social work*, 3rd edn, Basingstoke: Palgrave Macmillan.

Banks, S. (2007) 'Between equity and empathy: social professions and the new accountability', *Social Work and Society*, Special edition festschrift for Walter Lorenz, vol 5. Available at: www.socwork.net/2007/festschrift

Banks, S. (2009) 'Values and ethics in work with young people', in J. Hine and J. Wood (eds), *Work with young people: developments in theory, policy and practice*, London, Sage, pp 48–59.

—

Banks, S. (2012) *Ethics and values in social work,* 4th edn, Basingstoke: Palgrave Macmillan.

Banks, S. (2013) 'Negotiating personal engagement and professional accountability: professional wisdom and ethics work', *European Journal of Social Work,* forthcoming, DOI: 10.1080/13691457.2012.732931

Banks, S. and Gallagher, A. (2009) *Ethics in professional life: virtues for health and social care,* Basingstoke: Palgrave Macmillan.

Banks, S. and Nøhr, K. (eds) (2012) *Practising social work ethics around the world: cases and commentaries,* Abingdon: Routledge.

Barker, R.L. and Branson, D.M. (2000) *Forensic social work,* 2nd edn, Binghamton, NY: Haworth Press.

Barnard, A., Horner, N. and Wild, J. (2008) *The value base of social work and social care,* Maidenhead, Open University Press.

Barr, F. (2010) 'Contactpoint to be scrapped', *E-Health Insider.* Available at: www.ehi.co.uk/news/ehi/5903/contactpoint-to-be-scrapped

Barsky, A.E. (2009) *Ethics and values in social work: an integrated approach for a comprehensive curriculum,* New York: Oxford University Press.

Beckett, C. and Maynard, A. (2005) *Values and ethics in social work: an introduction,* London: Sage).

Blackledge, P. (2008) 'Marxism and ethics', *International Socialism* 2/120, pp 125–50. Available at: www.isj.org.uk/ (accessed March 2012).

Blackledge, P. (2012) *Marxism and ethics: freedom, desire and revolution,* New York: SUNY Press.

Boler, M. and Zembylas, M. (2003) 'Discomforting truths: the emotional terrain of understanding difference', in P. Trifonas (ed) *Pedagogies of difference: Rethinking education for social change,* New York: Routledge Falmer, pp 110–35.

Bouquet, B. (1999) 'De l'éthique personelle à une éthique professionelle', *EMPAN,* no 36, pp 27–33.

Bowles, W., Collingridge, M., Curry, S. and Valentine, B. (2006) *Ethical practice in social work: An applied approach,* Crow's Nest, New South Wales: Allen and Unwin.

—

Bozalek, V. (2011) 'Acknowledging privilege through encounters with difference: Participatory learning and action techniques for decolonizing methodologies in Southern contexts', *International Journal of Social Research Methodology*, vol 4, no 6, pp 465–80.

Bozalek, V. (2012) 'Interview with Nancy Fraser', *Social Work Practitioner/Researcher*, vol 24, no 1, pp 136–51.

Bozalek, V. and Boughey, C. (2012) '(Mis)framing higher education in South Africa', *Social Policy & Administration*, vol 46, no 6, pp 688–703.

Bozalek, V., Leibowitz, B., Carolissen, R. and Boler, M. (eds) (in press) *Discerning critical hope in educational practice*, London and New York: Routledge.

Brake, M. and Bailey, R. (eds) (1980) *Radical social work and practice*, London: Edward Arnold.

Burton, J. and van den Broek, D. (2009) 'Accountable and countable: Information management systems and the bureaucratization of social work', *Journal of British Social Work*, vol 39, pp 1326–42.

Charleton, M. (2007) *Ethics for social care in Ireland: philosophy and practice*, Dublin: Gill and Macmillan.

Clarke, J., Gewirtz, S. and McLaughlin, E. (eds) (2000a) *New managerialism, new welfare?*, London: Sage Publications.

Clarke, J., Gewirtz, S. and McLaughlin, E. (2000b) 'Reinventing the welfare state', in: J. Clarke, S. Gewirtz and E. McLaughlin (eds) *New managerialism, new welfare?*, London: Sage Publications., pp 1-26.

Clifford, D. and Burke, B. (2009) *Anti-oppressive ethics and values in social work*, Basingstoke: Palgrave Macmillan.

Congress, E., Black, P. and Strom-Gottfried, K. (eds) (2009) *Teaching social work ethics and values: a curriculum resource*, Alexandra, VA: Council on Social Work Education.

Coplan, A. (2010) 'Feeling without thinking: lessons from the ancients on emotion and virtue-acquisition', *Metaphilosophy*, vol 41, nos 1–2, pp 132–51

Corrigan, P. and Leonard, P. (1978) *Social work practice under capitalism: a Marxist approach*, London: Macmillan.

Cowden, S. and Singh, G. (2007) 'The "user": friend, foe or fetish? A critical exploration of user involvement in health and social care', *Critical Social Policy*, vol 27, no 1, pp 5-23.

Craigie, J. (2011) 'Thinking and feeling: moral deliberation in a dual-process framework', *Philosophical Psychology*, vol 24, no 1, pp 53–71

Critchley, S. (2007) *Infinitely demanding: ethics of commitment, politics of resistance*, London: Verso.

CSWE (Council on Social Work Education) (2009) *Educational policies and accreditation standards*, Alexandria, VA: CSWE.

Davidson, M. (2004) 'Bones of contention: Using self and story in the quest to professionalise higher education teaching – an interdisciplinary approach', *Teaching in Higher Education*, vol 9, no 3, pp 299–312.

Davis, M. (1999) *Ethics and the university*, London: Routledge.

Department for Education (2010) *Building a safe and confident future: one year on. Detailed proposals from the social work reform board*, London: Department for Education, www.education.gov.uk.

Department for Education, Department of Health and Home Office (2011) *Vetting and barring remodelling review – report and reccomendations, February 2011*, London: Home Office. Available at: www.homeoffice.gov.uk/publications/, accessed February 2011.

Derbyshire, J. (2012) '"We need to talk about Englishness": *New Statesman* profile of Stuart Hall', *New Statesman*, 24–30 August.

Dolgoff, R., Loewenberg, F. and Harrington, D. (2009) *Ethical decisions for social work practice*, 8th edn, Belmont, CA: Brooks Cole.

Dunleavy, P. and Hood, C. (1994) 'From old public administration to new public management', *Public Money and Management*, vol 14, no 3, pp 9-16.

Dunleavy, P., Margetts, H., Bastow, S. and Tinkler, J. (2006) 'New public management is dead – long live digital-era governance', *Journal of Public Administration Research and Theory*, vol 16, no 3, pp 467–94.

Dustin, D. (2007) *The McDonaldization of social work*, London: Ashgate.

Eagleton, T. (2011) *Why Marx was right*, Yale: Yale University Press.

Elkins, J. (2005) *Master narratives and their discontents*, New York: Routledge.

Emmet, D. (1962) 'Ethics and the social worker', *British Journal of Psychiatric Social Work*, vol 6, pp 165–72.

Ferguson, I. (2008) *Reclaiming social work: Challenging neo-liberalism and promoting social justice*, London: Sage.

Ferguson, I and Lavalette, M. (eds) (2009) 'Social work after Baby P: issues, debates and alternative perspectives', Liverpool: Liverpool Hope University Press.

Ferguson, I. and Woodward, R. (2009) *Radical social work in practice: Making a difference*. Bristol: Policy Press.

Flaker, V. (2012) *Programme of direct social work ethics*, Ljubljana, unpublished (for details of Occupy Ljubljana, see www.socialworkfuture.org/articles-and-analysis/international-articles/168-occupy-ljubljana).

Fraser, N. (1989) *Unruly practices: power, discourse and gender in contemporary social theory* Oxford: Polity Press.

Fraser, N. (2012) 'Social exclusion, global poverty and scales of (in) justice: rethinking law and poverty in a globalising world', in S. Liebenberg and Q. Quinot (eds) *Law and poverty: perspectives from South Africa and beyond*, Cape Town: Juta.

Freire, P. (2004) *Pedagogy of indignation*. Boulder, CO: Paradigm.

Galper, J. (1980) *Social work practice: a radical perspective*, Englewood Cliffs, US: Prentice Hall.

Gil, D.G. (1998) *Confronting injustice and oppression: concepts and strategies for social workers*, New York: Columbia University Press.

Graeber, D. (2011) *Debt: the first 5,000 years,* New York: Melville House.

Gray, M. and Webb, S. (eds) (2010) *Ethics and value perspectives in social work*, Basingstoke: Palgrave Macmillan.

Gronbjerg, K. and Salamon, L.M. (2002) 'Devolution, marketization and the changing shape of government-nonprofit relations', in L.M. Salamon (ed), *The state of nonprofit America*, Washington: Brookings Institution.

Gutierrez, L.M., Parsons, R.J. and Cox, E.O. (eds) (1998) *Empowerment in social work practice: a sourcebook*, Pacific Grove, CA: Brooks/Cole.

Harding, S. (2004) 'A socially relevant philosophy of science? Resource from standpoint theory's controversiality', *Hypatia*, vol 19, no 1, pp 25–47.

Harvey, D. (2005) *A brief history of neoliberalism*. Oxford: Oxford University Press.

Healy, K. (2009) 'A case of mistaken identity: The social welfare professions and the New Public Management', *Journal of Sociology*, vol 45, no 4, pp 401–18.

Hekman, S.J. (1995) *Moral voices, moral selves: Carol Gilligan and feminist moral theory*, Pennsylvania: Pennsylvania State University Press.

Houston-Vega, M.K., Nuehring, E.M. and Daguio, E.R. (1997) *Prudent practice: a guide for managing malpractice risk*, Washington, DC: NASW Press.

Hunt, L. (2007) *Inventing human rights: a history*, New York: Norton.

Ife, J. (2008) *Human rights and social work: towards rights-based practice*, revised edn, Cambridge, UK: Cambridge University Press.

IFSW (International Federation of Social Workers) (2010) Definition of social work, www.eassw.org/definition.asp (retrieved 6 June 2010).

IFSW (International Federation of Social Workers) and IASSW (International Association of Schools of Social Work) (2004) *Ethics in social work, statement of principles,* Berne: IFSW and IASSW. Available at: www.ifsw.org

Intemann, K. (2010) '25 years of feminist empiricism and standpoint theory: Where are we now?', *Hypatia*, vol 25, no 4, pp 778–96.

Ito, F. (2011) 'The rise and fall of professional social work in Japan: evolution, devolution and neoliberal turn?', *The Culture in Our Time*, no 123, pp 5-25.

Jani, J.S. and Reisch, M. (2011) 'Common human needs, uncommon solutions: Applying a critical framework to perspectives on human behavior', *Families in Society*, vol 92, no 1, pp 13–20.

Jordan, B. (2006) *Social policy for the twenty first century*, London, Polity Press.

Jordan, B. (2010) *Why the Third Way failed: economics, morality and the origins of the 'Big Society'*, Bristol, Policy Press.

Joseph, J. and Fernandes, G. (eds) (2006) *An enquiry into ethical dilemmas in social work*, Mumbai: College of Social Work, Nirmala Niketan.

Kamenka, E. (1969) *Marxism and ethics*, London: Macmillan.

Kelly, J.J. and Clark, E.J. (eds) (2009) *Social work speaks: National Association of Social Workers policy statements, 2009–2012,* Washington: NASW Press.

Kim, G. (2007) 'A critical comparison between a social justice perspective and a human rights perspective for the social work profession within a changing context', in *Human rights and social justice: rethinking social welfare's mission*, Seoul: Korean Academy of Social Welfare, pp 205–26.

Kirk, S.A. and Reid, W.J. (2002). *Science and social work*, New York: Columbia University Press.

Kosaki, H. (2011) 'The dominance of care management approach in Japan: the emergence of bio-politics under the Long Term Care Insurance Act', *The Culture of Our Times*, no 123, pp 27–43..

Kristjánsson, K. (2009) 'Putting emotion into the self: a response to the 2008 *Journal of Moral Education* Special Issue on moral functioning', *Journal of Moral Education*, vol 38, no 3, pp 255–70.

Langen, M. and Lee, P. (eds) (1989) *Radical social work today*, London: Unwin Hyman.

Lavalette, M. (ed) (2011) *Radical social work today: social work at the crossroads*. Bristol: Policy Press.

Levy, C.S. (1973) 'The value base of social work', *Journal of Education for Social Work*, vol 9, pp 34–42.

Levy, R. (2010) 'New public management: end of an era?', *Public Policy and Administration*, vol 25, no 2, pp 234–40.

Lingås, L. (1999) *Etik for social – og sundhedsarbejdere. En grundbog*, Copenhagen: Hans Reitzels Forlag.

Linzer, N. (1999) *Resolving ethical dilemmas for social work practice*, Needham Heights, MA: Allyn and Bacon.

Leonard, P. (1995) 'Postmodernism, socialism and social welfare', *Journal of Progressive Human Services*, vol 6, pp 3-19.

Leonard, P. (1997) *Postmodern welfare: reconstructing an emancipatory project,* London, Sage.

London Edinburgh Weekend Return Group (1980) *In and against the state*, London: Pluto Press.

Lukes, S. (1985) *Marxism and morality,* Oxford: Oxford University Press.

—

Lundy, C. (2004) *Social work and social justice,* 2nd edn, Toronto: University of Toronto Press.

Marx, K. (1975) *Capital,* London: Penguin.

Marx, K. and Engels, F. (1848/1969) 'Manifesto of the Communist Party', in L. Feuer (ed) *Marx and Engels: basic writings on politics and philosophy,* Glasgow: Collins/Fontana, pp 43–82.

McLeod, C. and Sherwin, S. (2000) 'Relational autonomy, self-trust, and health care for patients who are oppressed', in C. Mackenzie and N. Stoljar (eds) *Relational autonomy: feminist perspectives on autonomy, agency and the social self,* New York: Oxford University Press, pp 259–79.

McNally, D. (2011) *Global slump: the economics and politics of crisis and resistance,* Oakland, PM Press

Meagher, G. and Parton, N. (2004) 'Modernising social work and the ethics of care', *Social Work and Society,* vol 2, no 1, pp 10–27.

Mullaly, B. (1997) *Structural social work: ideology, theory, and practice,* Ontario, Canada: Oxford University Press.

Munro, E. (2011) *The Munro review of child protection – part 1: A systems analysis,* London: Department for Education. Available at www.education.gov.uk

Nakamura, Y. and Japanese Association of Social Workers (eds) (1999), *Social work ethics handbook,* Tokyo: Chuou-hoki.

Nakazawa, S. (2012) 'Care management practice', discussion paper presented to a workshop for care managers.

NASW (National Association of Social Workers) (1999) *Code of ethics,* Washington, DC: NASW.

NASW (2008) *Code of ethics,* revised edn, Washington, DC: NASW.

Newman, J. (2000) 'Beyond the new public management? Modernizing public services', in J. Clarke, S. Gewirtz and E. McLaughlin (eds) *New managerialism, new welfare?,* London: Open University/Sage, pp 45–61.

Newman, J. (2005) 'Participative governance and the remaking of the public sphere', in J. Newman (ed) *Remaking governance: peoples, politics and the public sphere,* Bristol: Policy Press, pp 119–38.

NVMW (Nederlanse Vereniging van Maatschappelijk Werkers) (1999) *Beroepscode voor de maatschappelijk werker*, Utrecht: NVMW.

NVMW (2010) *Beroepscode voor de maatschappelijk werker*, Utrecht: NVMW.

Orlie, M.A. (1997) *Living ethically: acting politically*, Ithaca: Cornell University Press.

Ortiz, L.O. and Jani, J.S. (2010) 'Critical race theory: A transformational model for teaching diversity', *Journal of Social Work Education*, vol 46, no 2, pp 175–93.

Parton, N. (2002) 'Postmodern and constructivist approaches to social work', in R. Adams, L. Dominelli and M. Payne (eds) *Social work: Themes, issues and debates*, 2nd edn, New York: Palgrave, pp 237–46.

Pease, B. (2009) 'From radical to critical social work: progressive transformation or mainstream incorporation?', in R. Adams, L. Dominelli and M. Payne (eds) *Critical practice in social work*, 2nd edn, Basingstoke: Palgrave, pp 189–98.

Philippart, F. (2012) 'Negotiating roles and boundaries: Introduction', in S. Banks and K. Nøhr (eds) *Practising social work ethics around the world: cases and commentaries*, London: Routledge, pp 32–8.

Plumwood, V. (1993) *Feminism and the mastery of nature*, London and New York: Routledge.

Progressive Social Work Network (Hong Kong) (2011) *Progressive social work manifesto*, Hong Kong, available at: www.socialworkfuture.org/articles-and-analysis/international-articles/230-progressive-social-work-manifesto (accessed May 2012).

Pullen-Sansfacon, A. and Cowden, S. (2012) *The ethical foundations of social work*, Harlow: Pearson-Longman.

Pumphrey, M.W. (1959) *The teaching of values and ethics in social work education*, vol 13, New York: Council on Social Work Education.

Rawls, J. (1971) *A theory of justice*, Cambridge: Cambridge University Press.

Reamer, F. (1993) *The philosophical foundations of social work*, New York: Columbia University Press.

Reamer, F. (1999) *Social work values and ethics*, New York: Columbia University Press.

Reamer, F. (2003) *Social work malpractice and liability: strategies for prevention*, 2nd edn, New York: Columbia University Press.

Reamer, F. (2006a) *Ethical standards in social work: a review of the NASW Code of Ethics*, 2nd edn, Washington, DC: NASW Press.

Reamer, F. (2006b) *Social work values and ethics*, 3rd edn, New York: Columbia University Press.

Reamer, F. (2013) *Social work values and ethics,* 4th edn, New York: Columbia University Press.

Reeser, L.C. and Epstein, I. (1990) *Professionalization and activism in social work*, New York: Columbia University Press.

Reisch, M. (2008) 'From melting pot to multiculturalism: The impact of racial and ethnic diversity on social work and justice in the United States', *British Journal of Social Work*, vol 38, no 4, pp 788–804.

Reisch, M. (2009) 'Die politik der soziale arbeit in zeiten der globalizierung', in F. Kessl and H.-U. Otto (eds) *Soziale arbeit ohne wohlfahrtsstaat? Zeitdiagnosen, problematisierungen und perspektiven*, Weinheim, Germany: Juventa, pp 223–44.

Reisch, M. and Andrews, J.L. (2001) *The road not taken: a history of radical social work in the United States*, Philadelphia: Brunner-Routledge.

Rogerson, M.D., Gottlieb, M.C., Handelsman, M.M., Knapp, S. and Younggren, J. (2011) 'Nonrational processes in ethical decision making', *American Psychologist*, vol 66, no 7, pp 614–23.

Rouzel, J. (1997) *Le travail d'éducateur spécialisé: Éthique et practique*, Paris: Dunod.

Sandlin, J.S. and Clark, M.C. (2009) 'From opportunity to responsibility: Political master narratives, social policy, and success stories in adult literacy education', *Teachers College Record*, vol 111, no 4, pp 999–1029.

Scottish Social Services Council (SSSC) (2009) *Codes of Practice for Social Service Workers and Employers*, Dundee: SSSC. Available at: www.sssc.uk.com/doc_details/1020-sssc-codes-of-practice-for-social-service-workers-and-employers

Sevenhuijsen, S. (1998) *Citizenship and the ethics of care: feminist considerations on justice, morality and politics*, London: Routledge.

Smith, D. (1990) *Texts, facts and femininity: Eexploring the relations of ruling*, New York, New York: Routledge.

Soss, J., Fording, R.C. and Schram, S.F. (2011) *Disciplining the poor: neoliberal paternalism and the persistent power of race*, Chicago: University of Chicago Press.

South African Council for Social Service Professions, Policy Guidelines for the Course of Conduct, Code of Ethics and the Rules for Social Workers. Available at: www.sacssp.co.za/website/wp-content/uploads/2012/06/Code-of-Ethics.pdf (accessed 30 August 2012).

Spufford, F. (2011) *Red plenty*, London: Faber & Faber.

SWAN (Social Work Action Network) (2004) *Social work and social justice: A manifesto for a new engaged practice*. Available at: www.socialworkfuture.org/about-swan/national-organisation/manifesto (accessed May 2012).

Thyer, B.A. (2007) 'Evidence-based practice in the US', in B.A. Thyer and M.A.F. Kazi (eds) *International perspectives on evidence-based practice in social work*, Birmingham: Venture Press.

Thompson, N, (2000) *Understanding social work: prepare for practice,* London: Palgrave.

Timmer, S. (ed) (1998) *Tijd voor ethiek. Handreikingen voor ethische vragen in de praktijk maatschappelijk werkers*, Bussum: Uitgeverij Coutinho.

Timms, N. (1983) *Social work values: an enquiry*, London: Routledge and Kegan Paul.

Tronto, J. (1993). *Moral boundaries: A political argument for an ethic of care*, New York and London: Routledge.

Tronto, J. (2010) 'Creating caring institutions: politics, plurality, and purpose', *Ethics and Social Welfare*, vol 4, no 2, pp 158–71.

Tronto, J.C. (2013) *Caring democracy: markets, equality and justice*, New York: New York University Press.

Truitt, W. (2005) *Marxist ethics: a short exposition*, New York: International Publishers.

Vetlesen, A.J. (1994) *Perception, empathy and judgment: an inquiry in the preconditions of moral performance*, University Park: Pennsylvania State University Press.

Walker, M.U. (1998) *Moral understandings: a feminist study of ethics*, New York: Routledge.

Webb, S.A. (2001) 'Some considerations on the validity of evidence-based practice in social work', *British Journal of Social Work*, vol 31, no 1, pp 57–79.

Weinberg, M. (2006) 'Pregnant with possibility: The paradoxes of "help" as anti-oppression and discipline with a young single mother', *Families in Society*, vol 87, no 2, pp 161–9.

Weinberg, M. (2009) 'Moral distress: A missing but relevant concept for ethics in social work', *Canadian Social Work Review*, vol 26, no 2, pp 139–52.

Weinberg, M. (2010) 'The social construction of social work ethics: Politicizing and broadening the lens', *Journal of Progressive Human Services*, vol 21, no 1, pp 32–44.

White, S., Wastell, D., Broadhurst, K. and Hall, C. (2010) 'When policy o'erleaps itself: The "tragic tale" of the integrated children's system', *Critical Social Policy*, vol 30, no 3, pp 405–29.

Wilken, J.P. (2010) *Recovering care: A contribution to a theory and practice of good care*, Amsterdam: SWP Publishers.

Yokoyama, T. et al (2011) *The position of social action and its educational effect: an examination for the welfare vision of social workers in Japan*, Kanazawa: University of Kanazawa Online Press

Young, I.M. (1990) *Justice and the politics of difference*, Princeton, New Jersey: Princeton University Press.

Young, I.M. (1997) 'Asymmetrical reciprocity: on moral respect, wonder and enlarged thought', *Constellations*, vol 3, no 3, pp 340–63.

Young, I.M. (2011) *Responsibility for justice*, Oxford: Oxford University Press.

Younghusband, E. (1967) *Social work and social values,* London: Allen and Unwin.

Lightning Source UK Ltd.
Milton Keynes UK
UKHW020634170722
405956UK00009B/511

9 781447 316183